Eliminate the Photoshop CS5 Learning Curve with Plug-ins and Actions

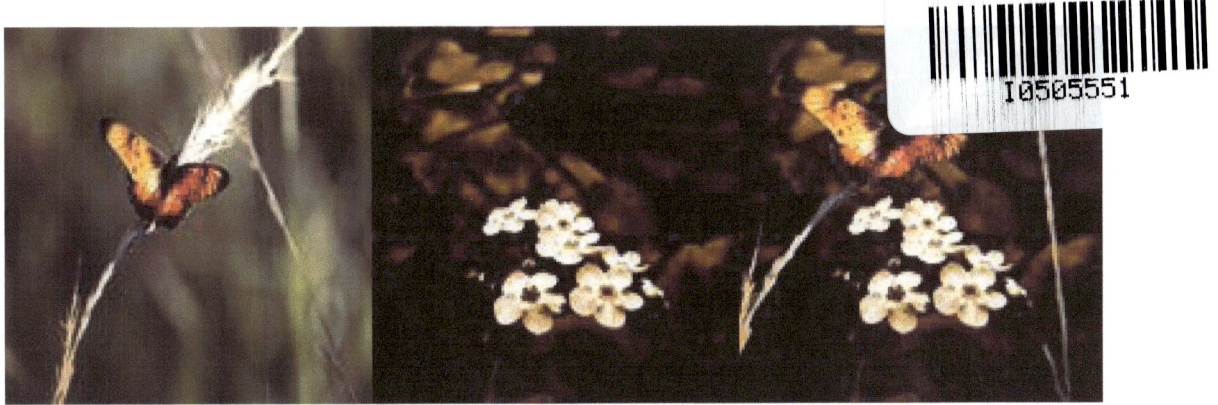

This book has been published as a Fund Raiser for the

The National Alzheimer's Association and

The Cystic Fibrosis Foundation

In Memory and Honor of wife

Dorothy A Bearden and Granddaughter Lindsey Fellows

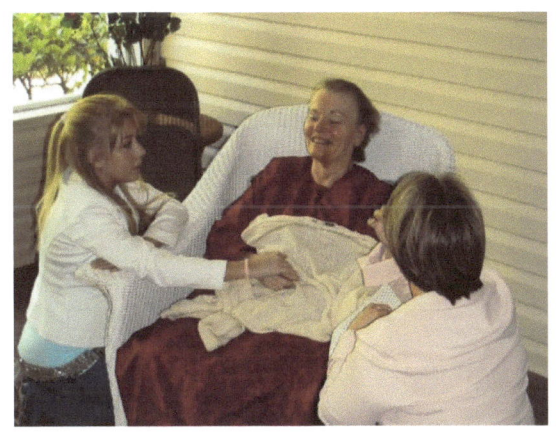

A SPECIAL THANKS TO THE FOLLOWING

Software Companies and Professional Photographer for their help and contributions

onOne Software Company
http://www.ononesoftware.com/

Topaz Labs
http://www.topazlabs.com/

Panos FX
http://www.panosfx.com/

Professional Photographer Rick Sellick
http://rick-sellick.smugmug.com/

OTHER PLUG-IN SOFTWARE COMPANIES USED ON PHOTOS INCLUDED IN THIS BOOK ARE:

Alien Skin Snap Art

Nik Software

INTRODUCTION

Adobe Elements, through their 12th major release, Photoshop CSd5 offers both amateur and professional photographers a maze of tools to enhance and adjust their photographs. Everything from Menus to toolbars giving you quick access to a variety of options to edit your image. The longer your work to learn how everything is used to make all of the adjustments available the sooner you come to realize that each major change requires several steps. These steps take time and for the professional it slows down his workflow. For the beginner it becomes a huge learning curve, and for older photographers that have found that their memory is not what it used to be, it become a real challenge to remember all of the difference steps involved needed to create that perfect picture.

After learning how to use Elements I advanced to Photoshop CS5 which in reality is a bundle of magic or so it seems to your friends that view your end results. I spent hours watching tutorials both on line and with CDs learning how to use this marvelous software, only to find out that there are shortcuts to accomplish what had been taking me so long to do the hard way. I am talking about third-party software known as plug-in modules. By installing software from companies like Nik Software, onOne Software, Topaz Labs, Ailen Skin, and Actions like Panos FX which is another series of plug-ins. A Photoshop action is a recording of a sequence of commands and operations that you can save and access later on. For those unfamiliar with Photoshop actions, they're simply pre-recorded tasks that you can save and reuse anytime. Installing a Photoshop action for more recent versions of Photoshop is easy: simply drag the .atn file onto the Actions palette or place it directly inside your *Adobe Photoshop\Presets\Photoshop Actions* folder. You can purchase these action sequences or create your own in Photoshop. You will soon learn that you have shortened that learning curve and increased your work flow.

This book is just a series of original photos and photos showing how you can make so many different adjustments and enhancements by using the third party software listed above. You don't have to work harder, just smarter. It's easy and a world of fun to see the art work you can create.

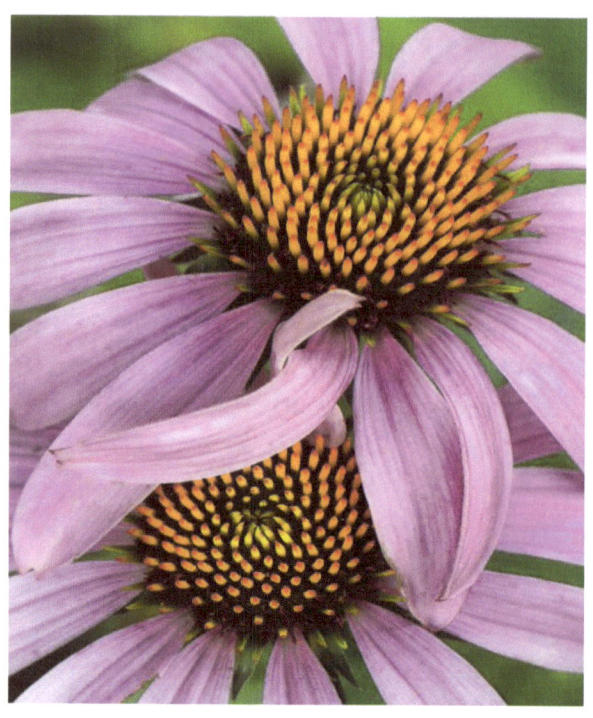

Original Photo

Photoshop CS5, Photo Tools 2.5, Johnny Hugs, Presets, Plug-In

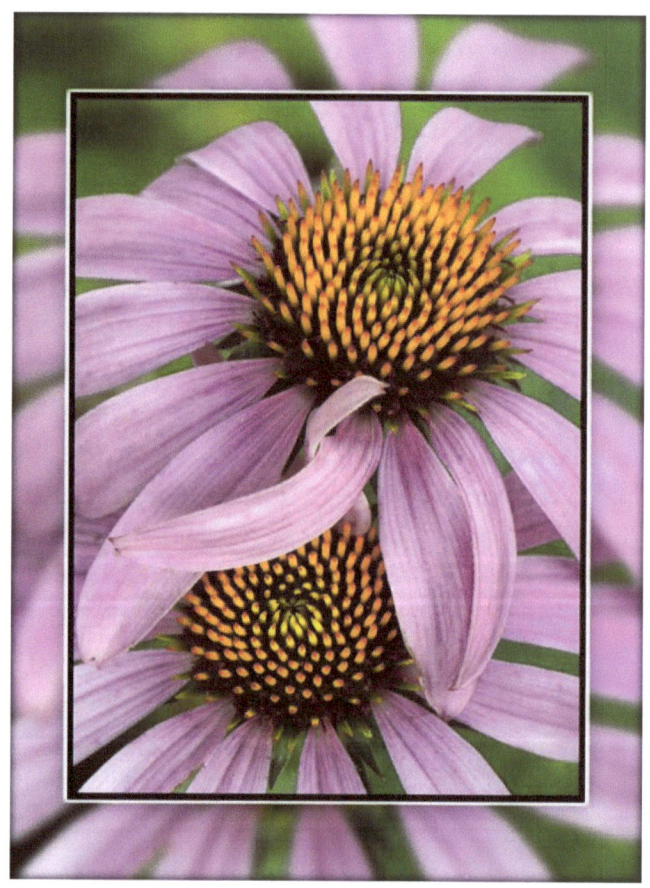

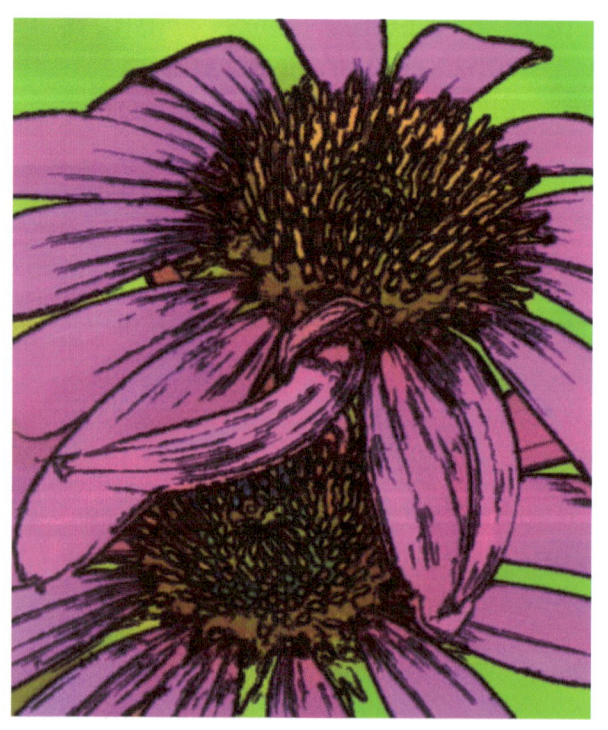

Photoshop CS5, Topaz Labs, Simplify 3, Cartoon, Plug-In

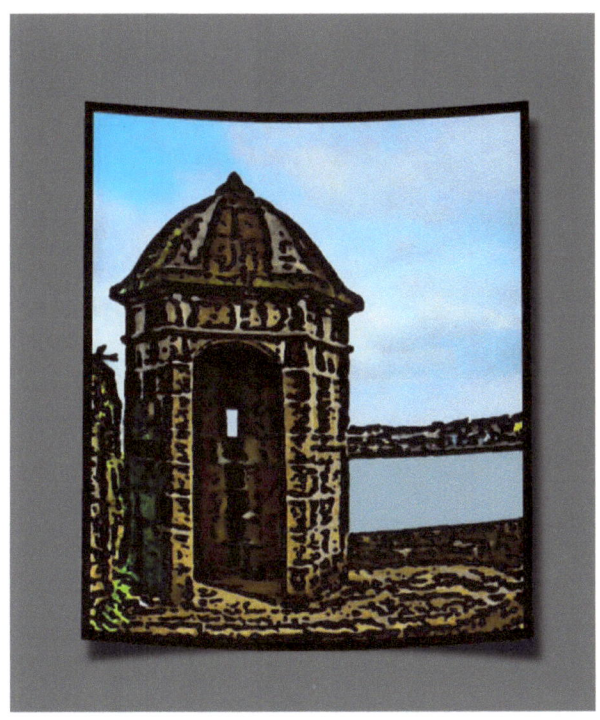

Photoshop CS5, PanosFx, PFx Effects, Actions, Topaz Labs, Watercolor/Comic, Plug-Ins

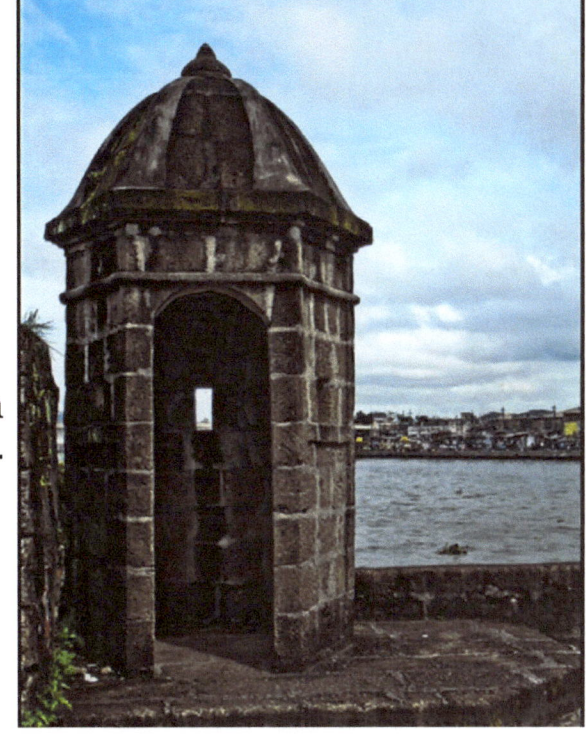

Photoshop CS5, onOne Software, Photo Tools 2.5,Kevin Kabota, Enter the Dragon, Plug-In

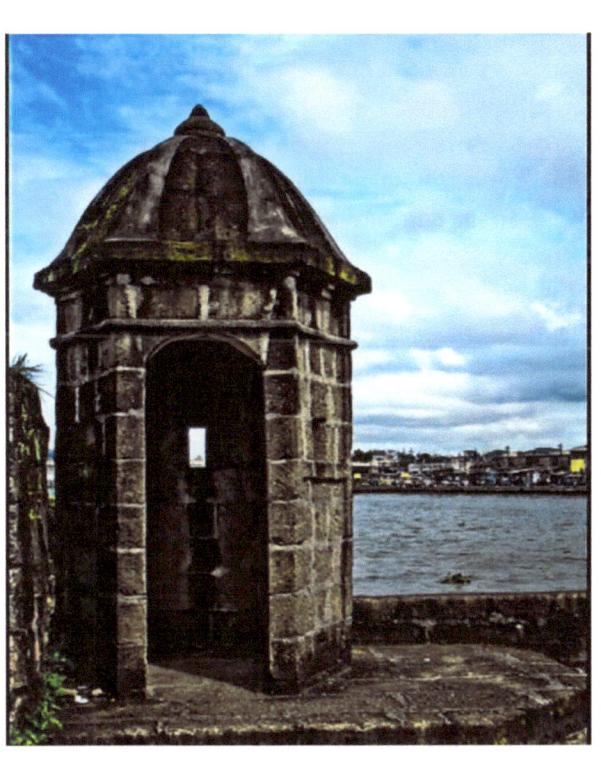

Photoshop CS5, Nik Software, Color Efex Pro 3.0, Contrast Color Range, Plug-In

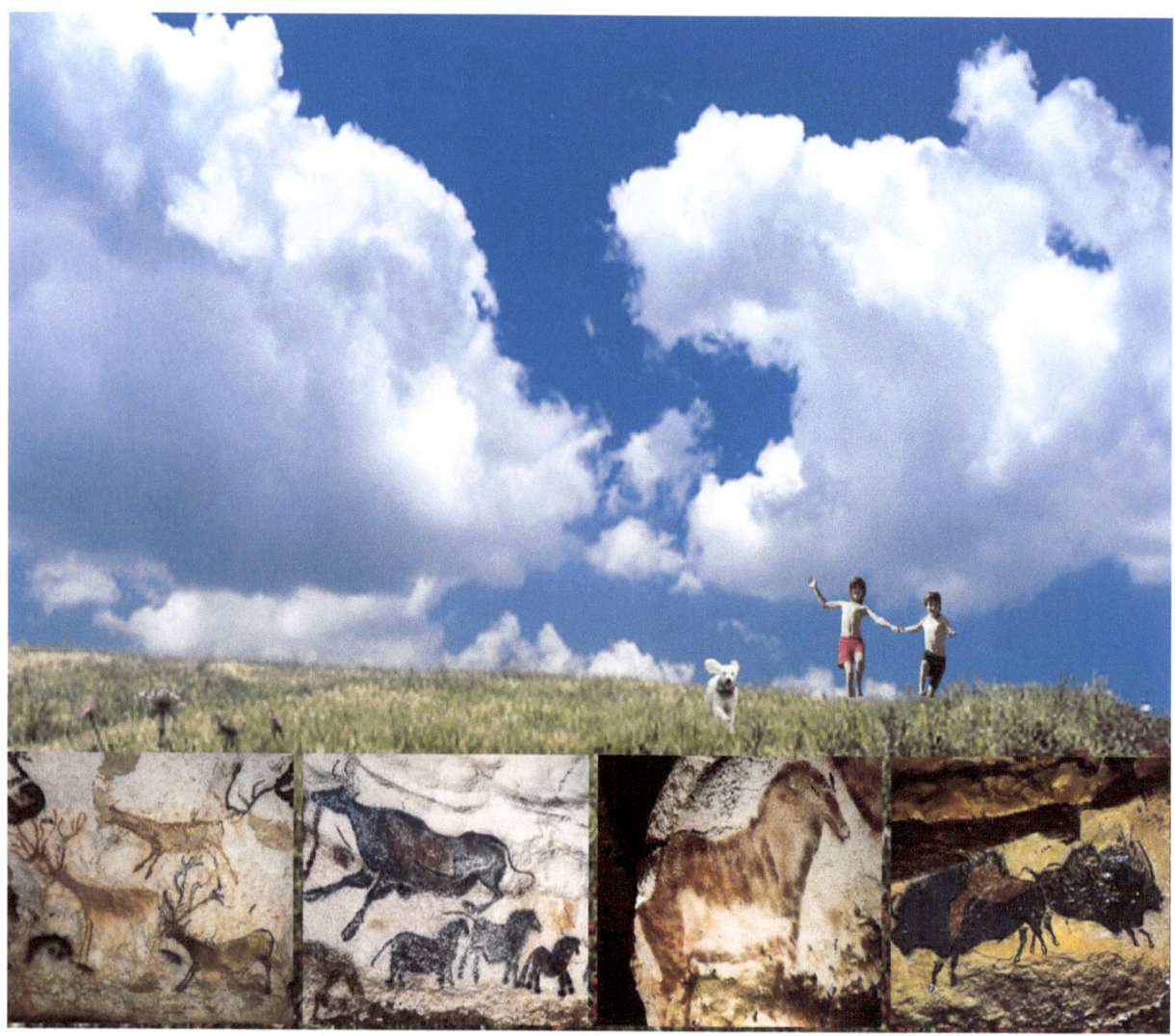

September 12, 1940, a warm afternoon in Southwestern France was the setting for the discovery of the Century. As two schoolboys hunted rabbits on a ridge covered with pine, oak, and blackberry brambles, their dog chases a rabbit down a hole beside a downed tree. Widening the hole, removing rocks, the boys follwed their dog and entered not merely another world, but another time. Underground, they discovered a "Versilles of prehistory;" a series of caves, today known as Lascaux, boasting wall paintings up to 18,000 years old. They saw on the walls what is shown above. It was like an encounter of a vanished people; a Cro-Magnon tribe that lived in this cave and recorded on the walls paintings that to this day have not faded with time.

Photoshop CS5, Quick Selection Tool, Nik Software Dfine 2 to eliminate noise, was needed along with seven different photos to tell the story that was written below the photos.

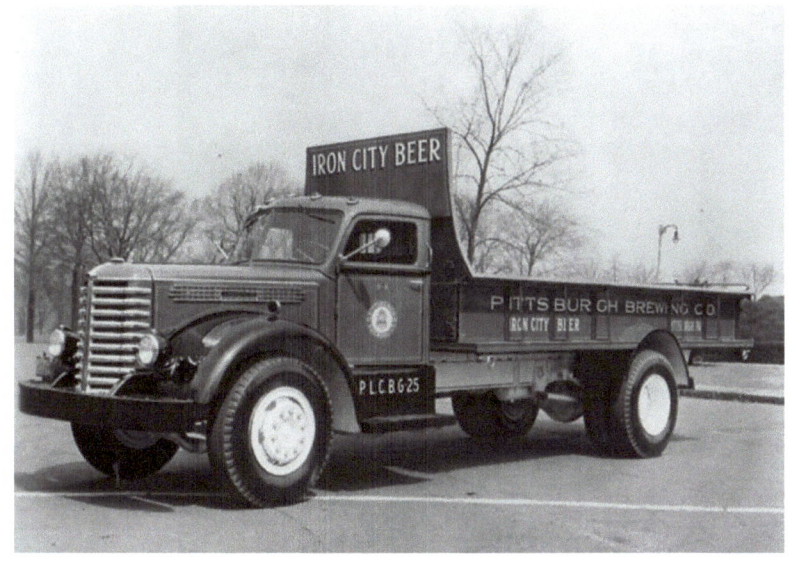

Original B&W photo taken in 1948

Photoshop CS 5
Nik Software Define
2.0Color Efex Pro 3.5
Bi Color effect, Plug-In

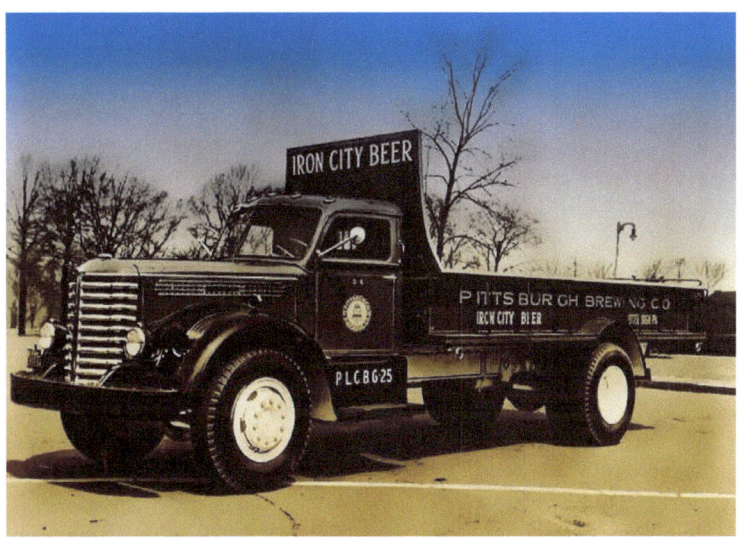

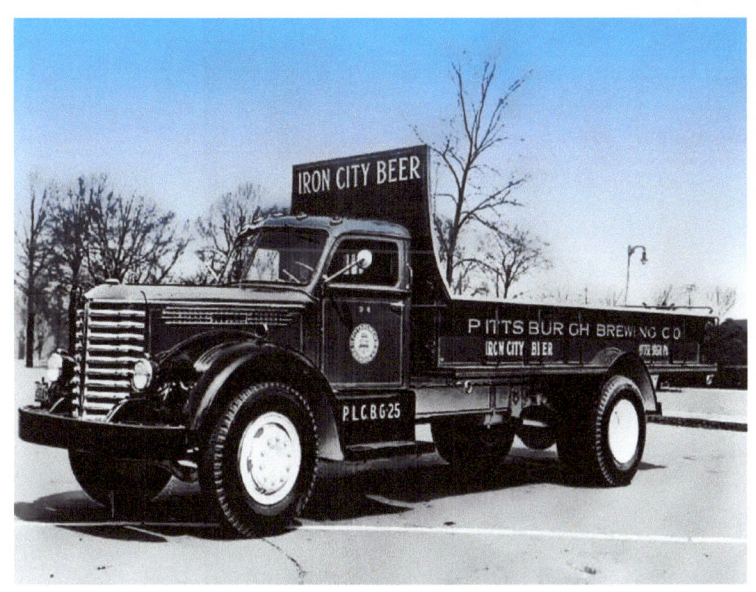

Photoshop CS5
Nik Software Define 2.0
Color Efex Pro 3.5
Kodachrome 64
Film Effect, Plug-In

Color Variations

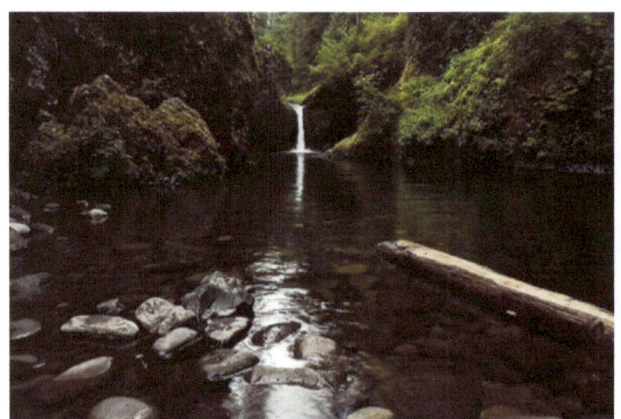

Original Photo

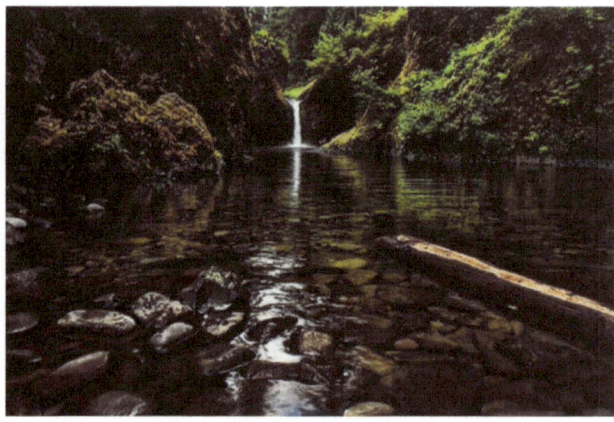

Photoshop CS5 Topaz Labs, Adjust 4, DeNoise 5, onOne Software, Photo Tools 2.5, Plug-Ins, Presets

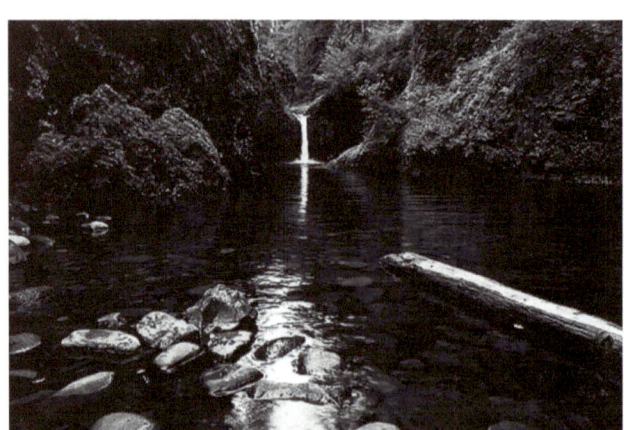

**Photoshop CS5
Nik Software
Silver Efex Pro, Plug-Ins**

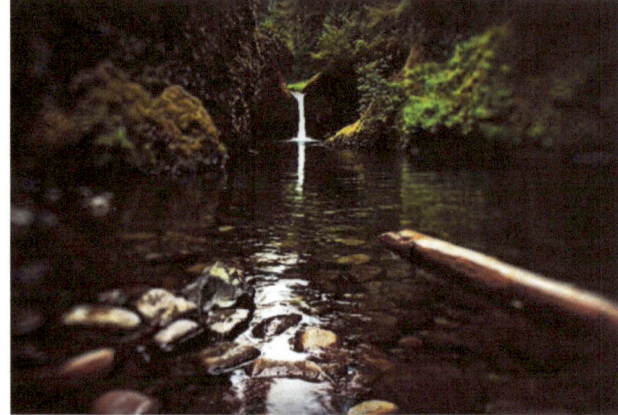

**Photoshop CS5
onOne Software
Focal Point 2, Plug-Ins**

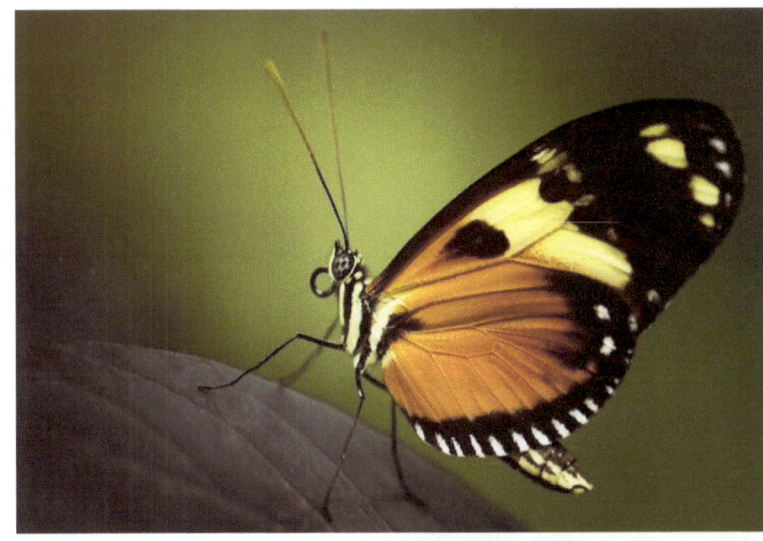

Close up shot processed and enhanced with Photoshop CS5

Close up shot processed and enhanced in Photoshop CS5

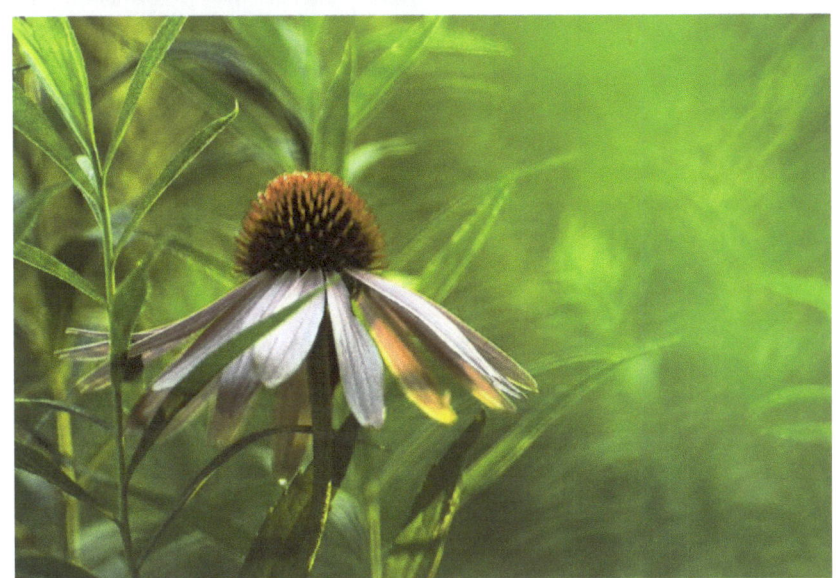

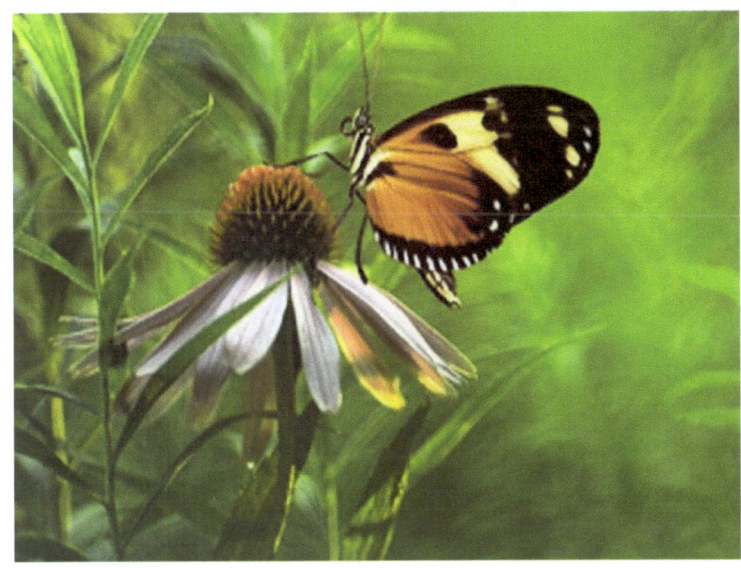

Photoshop CS5 using Quick Selection Tool and moving Butterfly to close up photo of the flower.

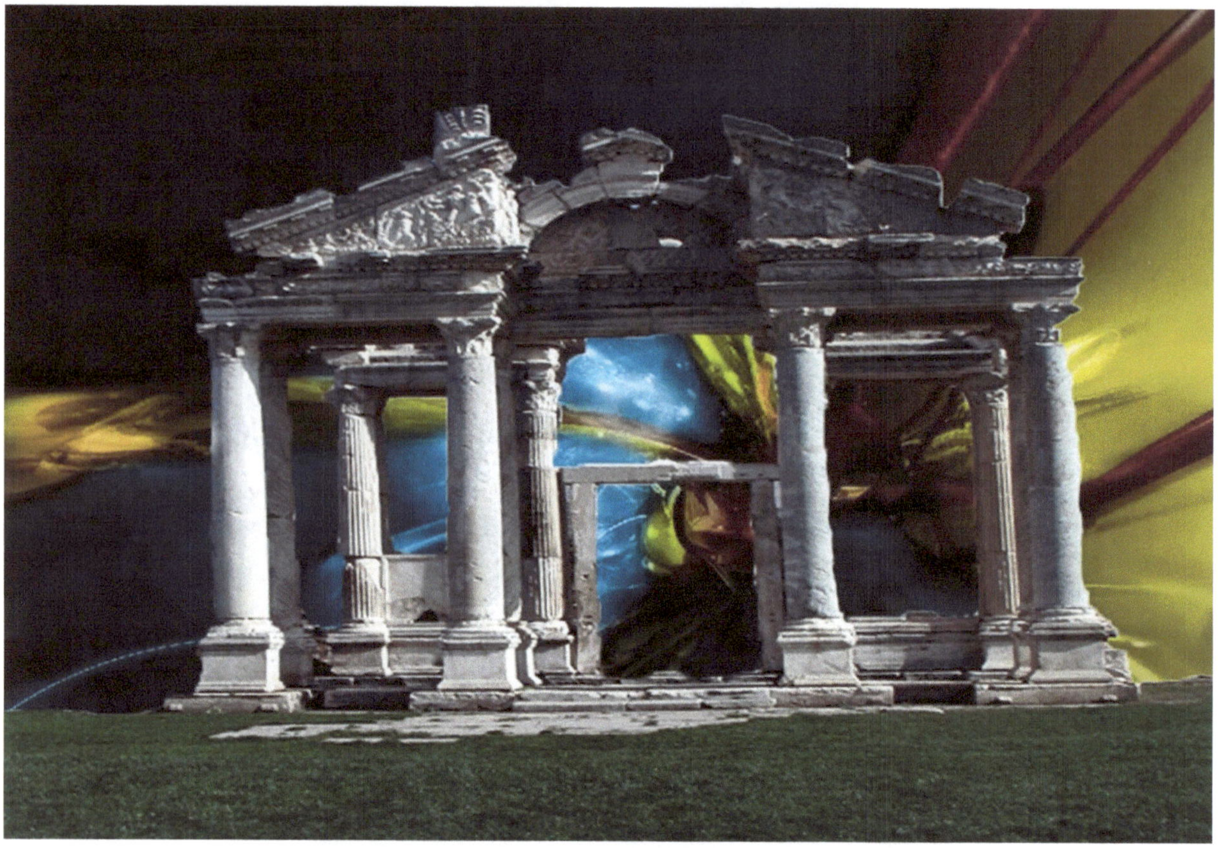

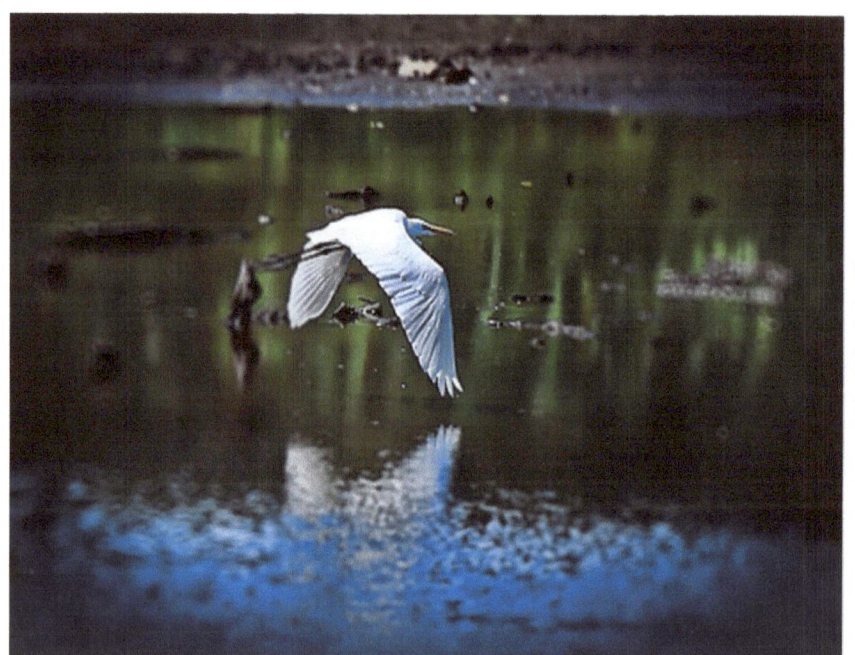

**Entrance to Temple of Aphrodite photo
and merged graphic art photo
Photoshop CS5
Quick Selection Tool & Eraser**

**Photoshop CS5
onOne Software
Focal Point 2,
Photo Tools 2.5
Preset**

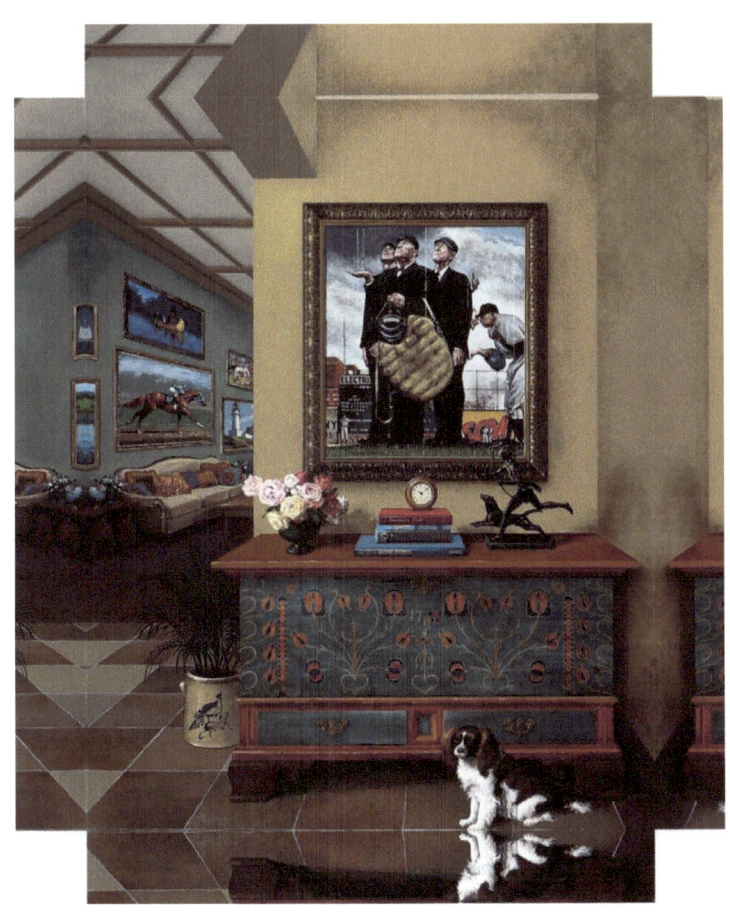

Jenness painting of Norman Rockwell painting.

onOne Software Photo Frame 4.5, Wrap Around

Peter Max painting onOne Software Photo Frame 4.5, Wrap Around

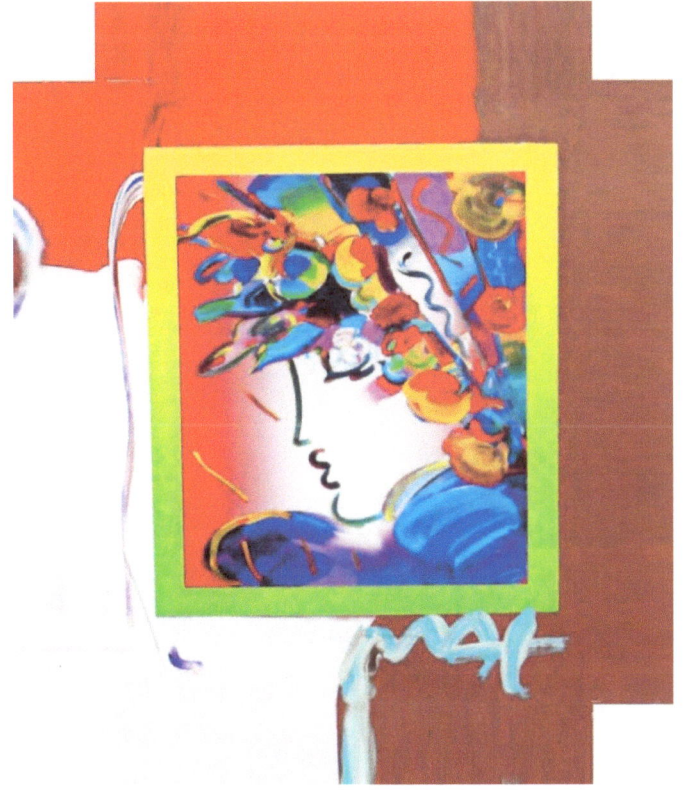

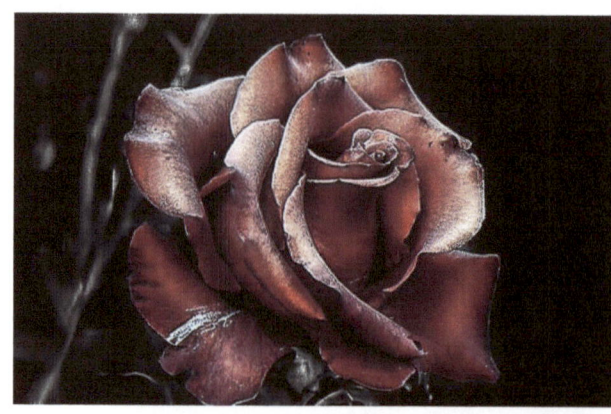

Topaz Labs Adjust 4 Plug-In

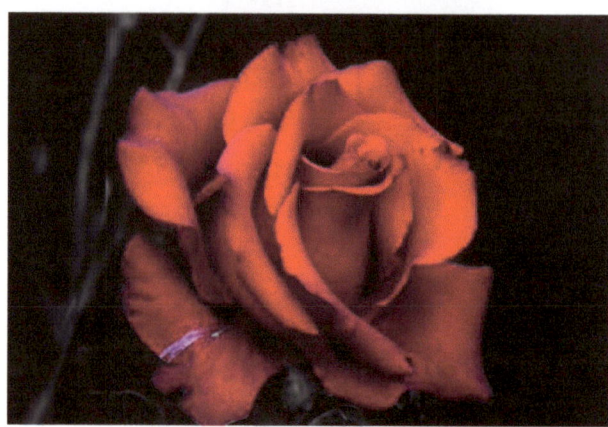

onOne Software Plug-In,Presets

Adobe Photoshop CS5

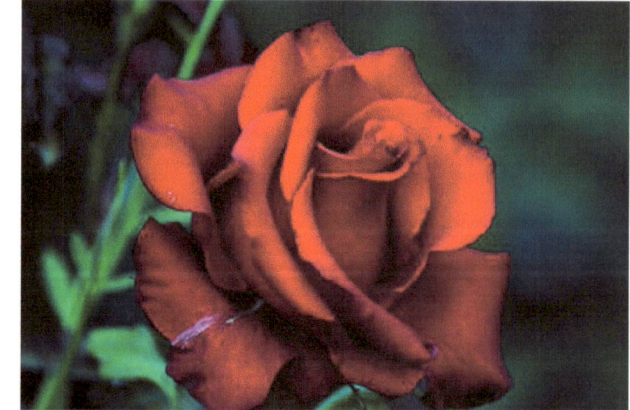

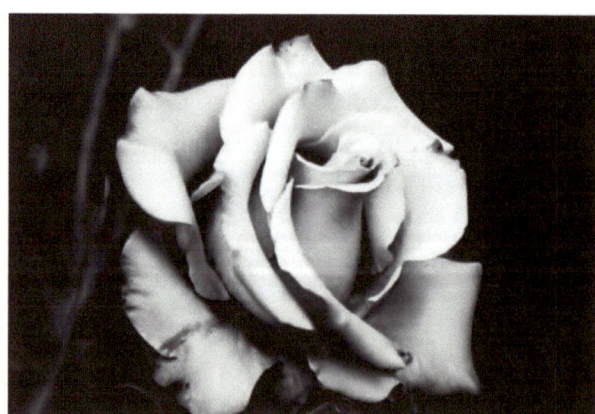

Nik Software

Silver Efex Pro

Plug-In

The top left image was a scanned magazine photo. Notice the texture in the lamp and picture frame.

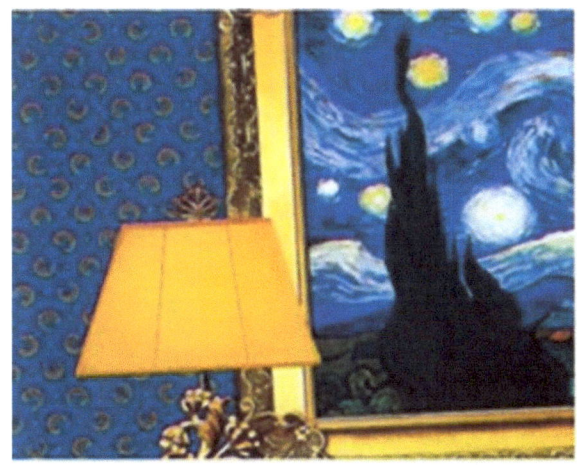 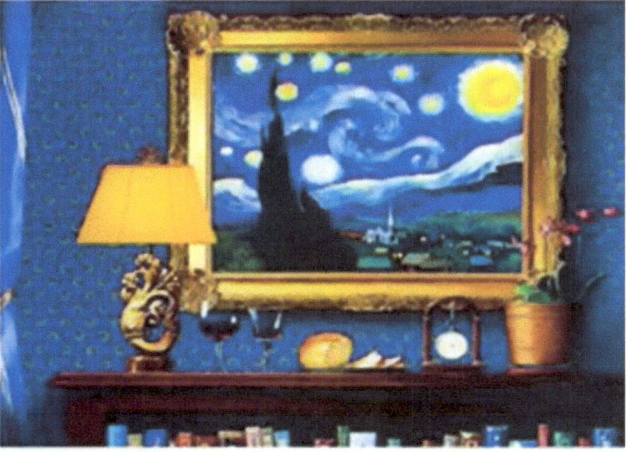

Photoshop CS5, Nik Software Define 2.0, onOne Software, Photo Tools 2.5 softens the texture of the original photo.

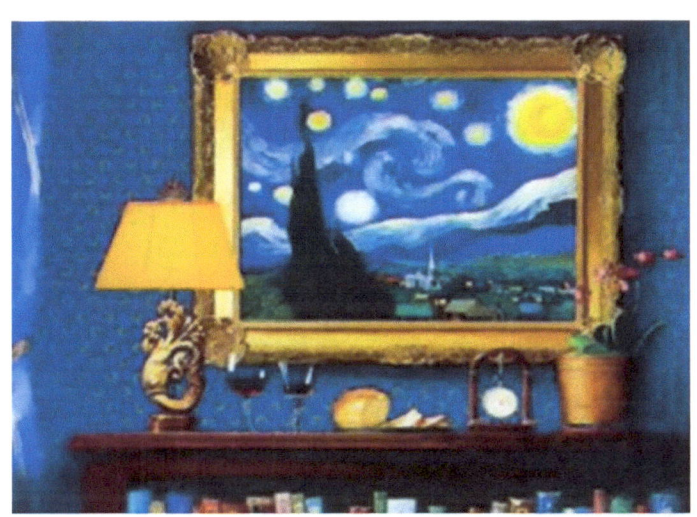

Photoshop CS5, Alien Skin Snap Art, Oil Painting effect, Plug-In

Photoshop CS5, Topaz Labs DeNoise 5, Adjust 4, Simplify 3, Plug-In

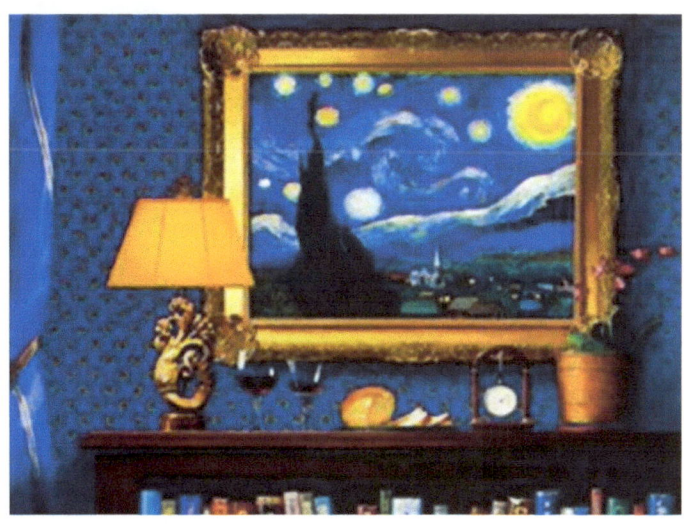

Original Photograph

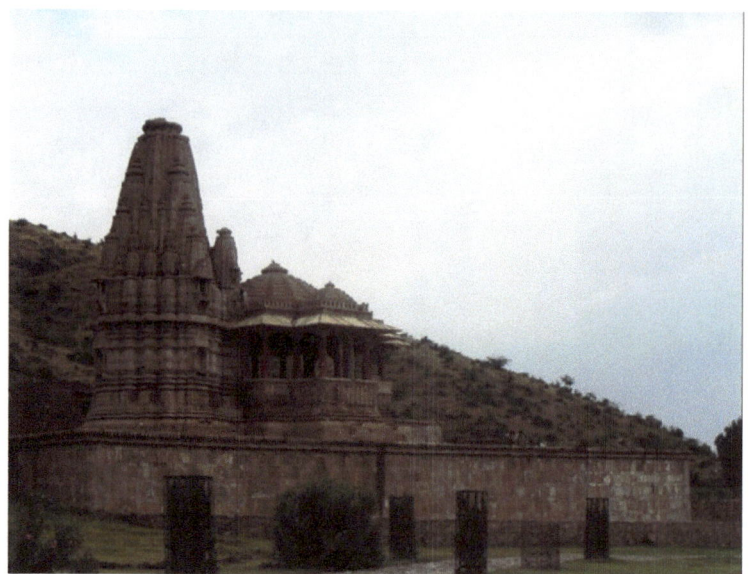

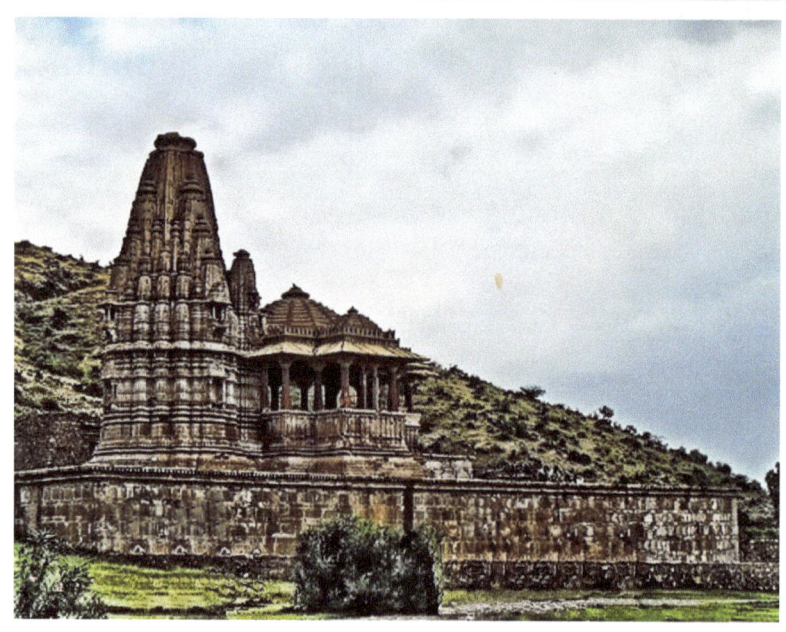

**Photoshop CS5
Photo Healing
BrushContent
AwareonOne
SoftwarePhoto Tools
2.5 Preset,Plug-In**

**Alien Skin Software
Alien Skin Snap Art 2
Oil Painting, Plug-In**

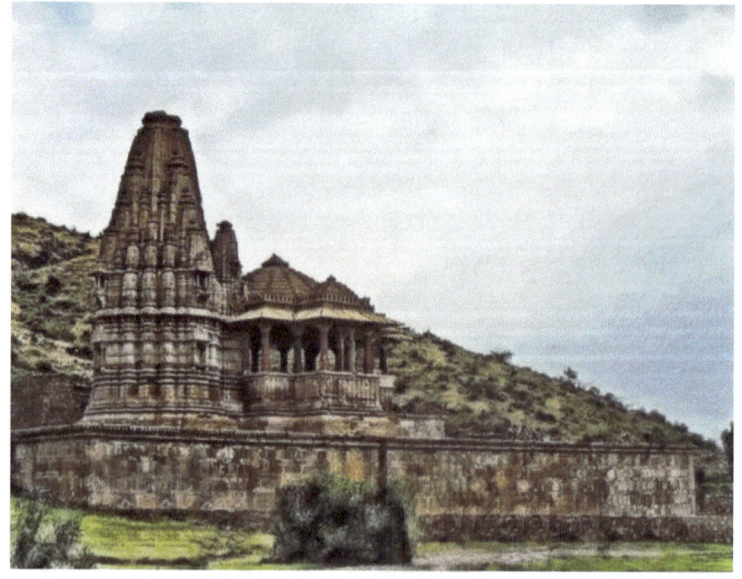

Adjustments to old photograph by Alfred Stieglits in NY city

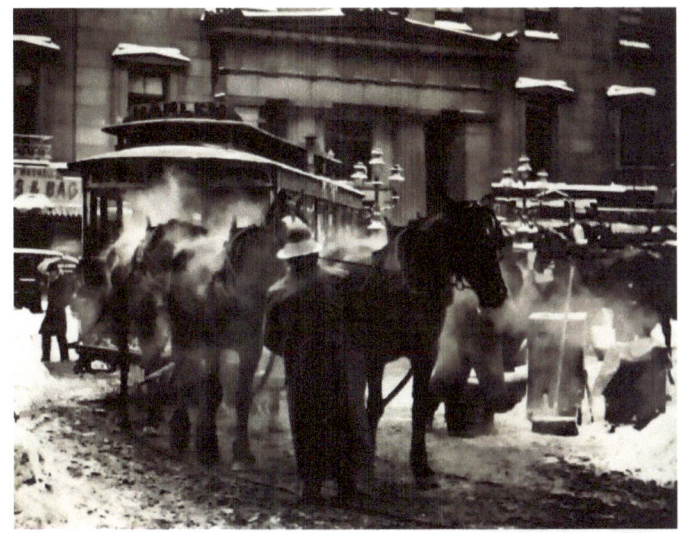

**Photoshop CS5
Nik Software Define 2
onOne Software Photo Tools
2.5, Presets,Plug-In**

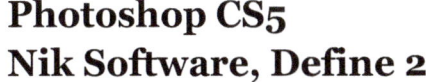

**Photoshop CS5
Nik Software, Define 2**

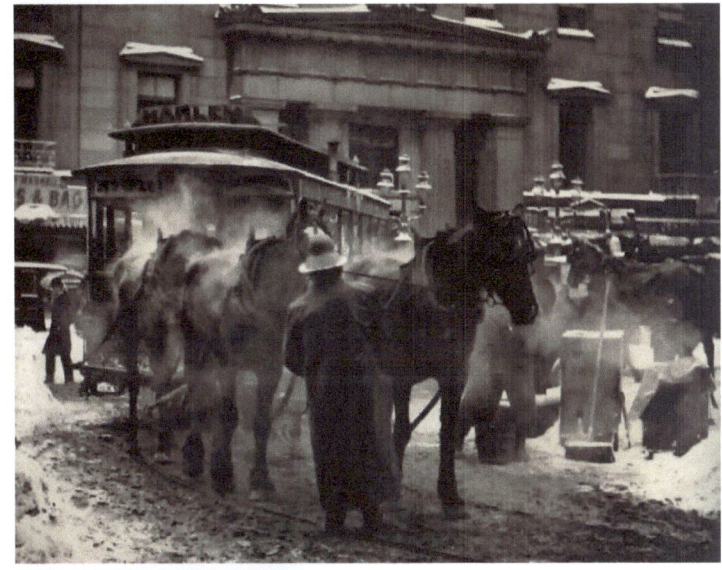

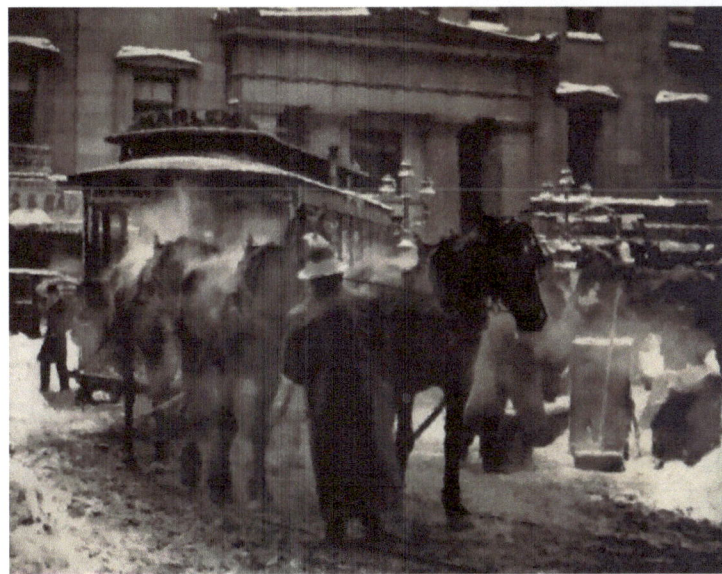

**Photoshop CS5
Ailen Skin Snap Art
Impasto oil painting
with small brush and
strokes for added
realism with no canvas
effect**

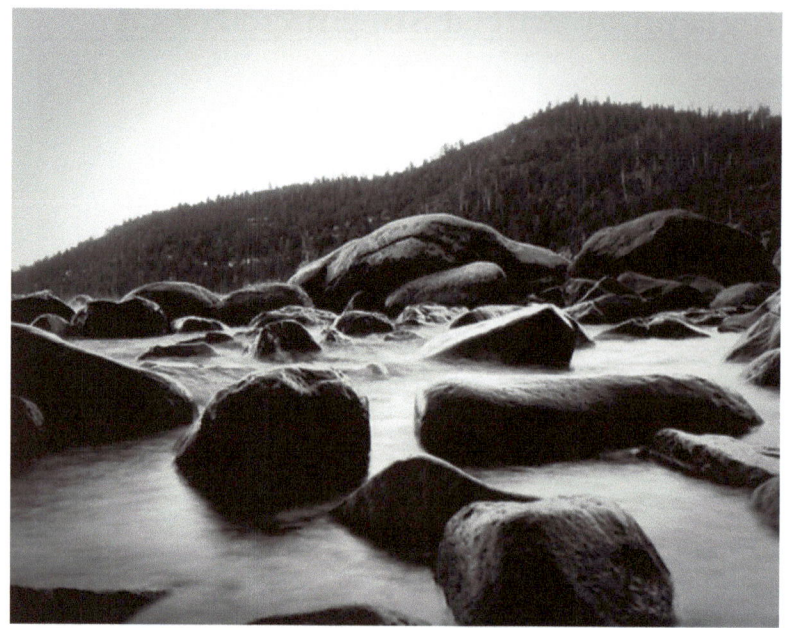

Original Photo

Photoshop CS5, onOne Software, Photo Tools 2.5, bottom half was enhanced and cut and merged to give both black & white and color

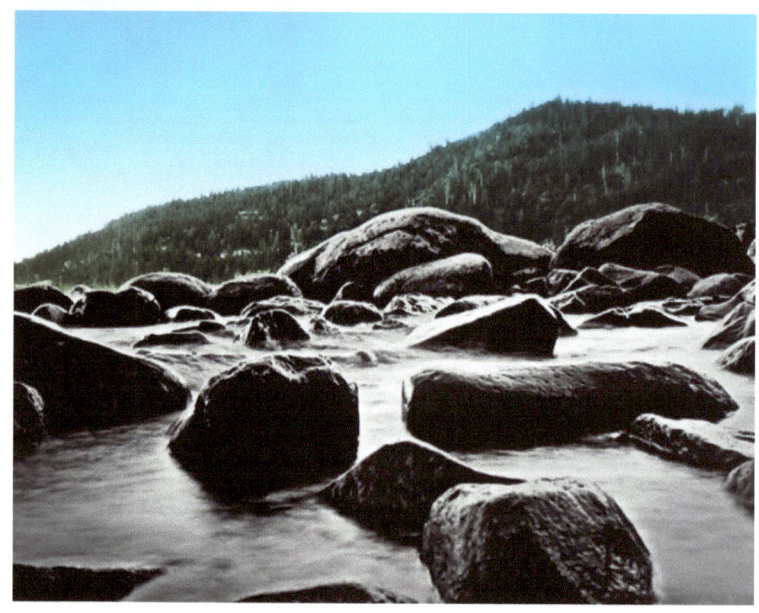

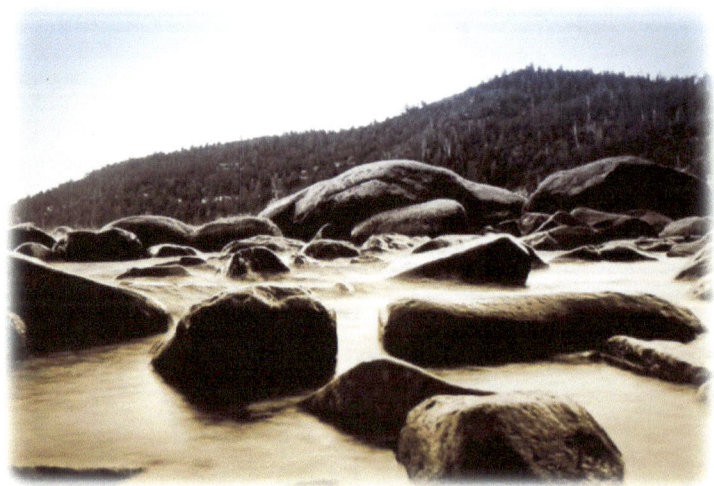

Photoshop CS5, onOne Software, Photo Tools 2.5, 1974 Preset, Plug-In

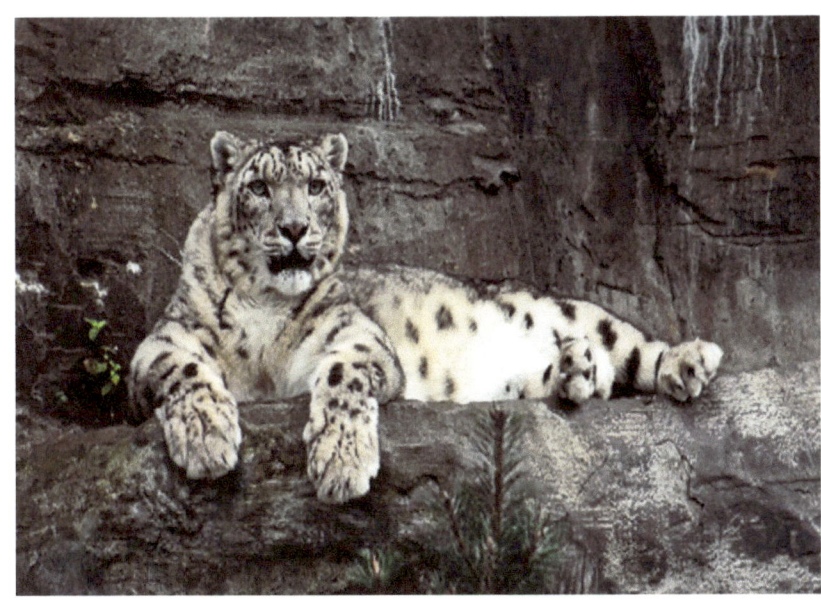

Original Photo

Photoshop CS5, onOne Software, Photo Frame 4.5, Photo Tools 2.5 Preset for enhancement, Plug-In

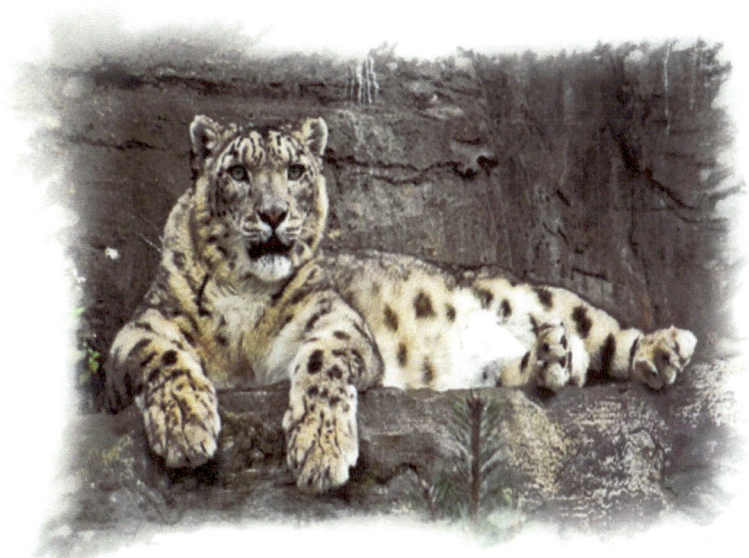

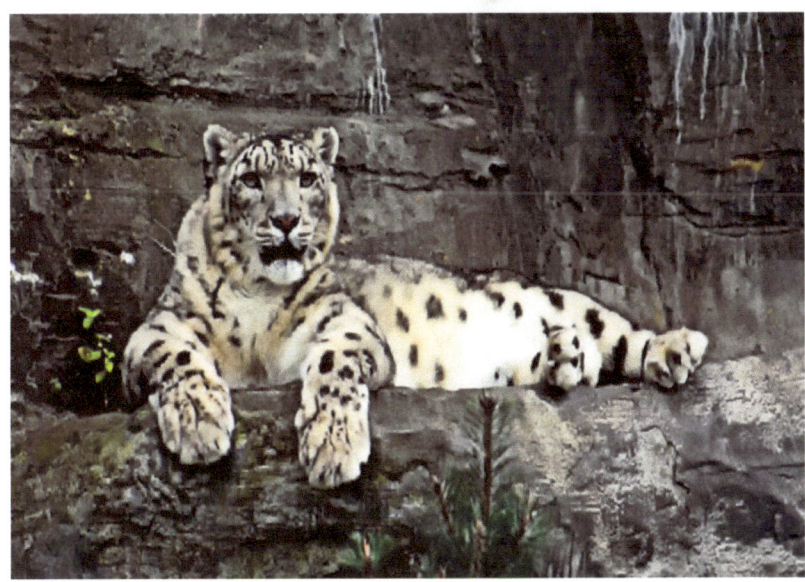

Photoshop CS5, onOne Software, Photo Tools 2.5, Image Optimizer Preset, Plug-In

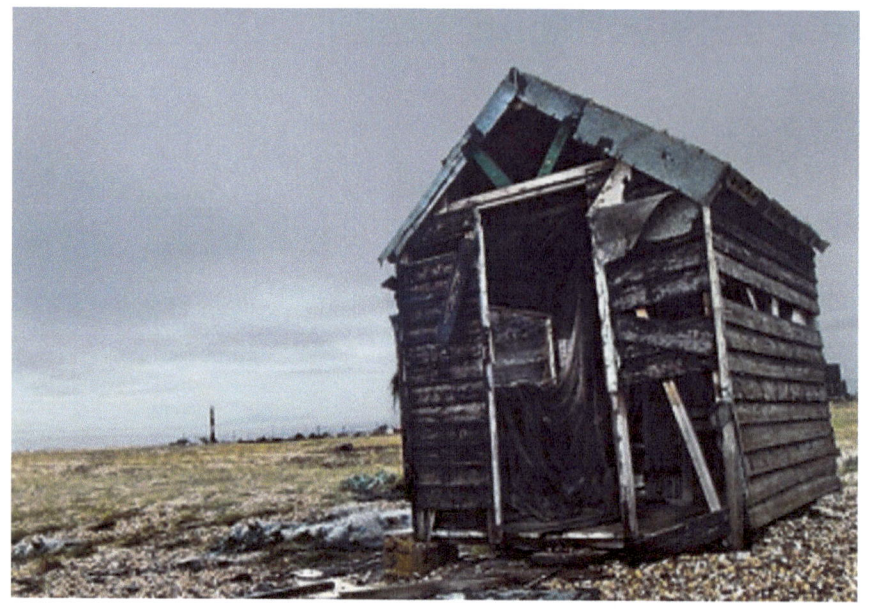

Original Photo

Photoshop CS5, Actions, Panos FX Book, Plug-In

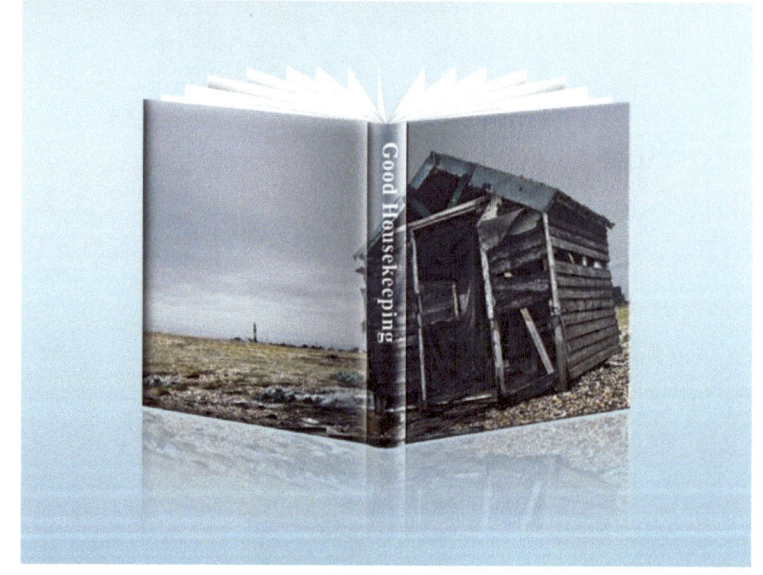

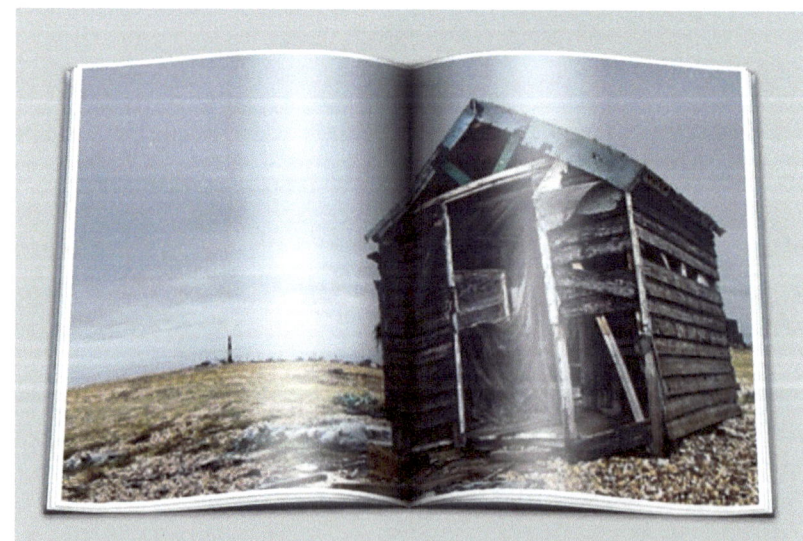

Photoshop CS5, Actions, Panos FX Analysis, Plug-In

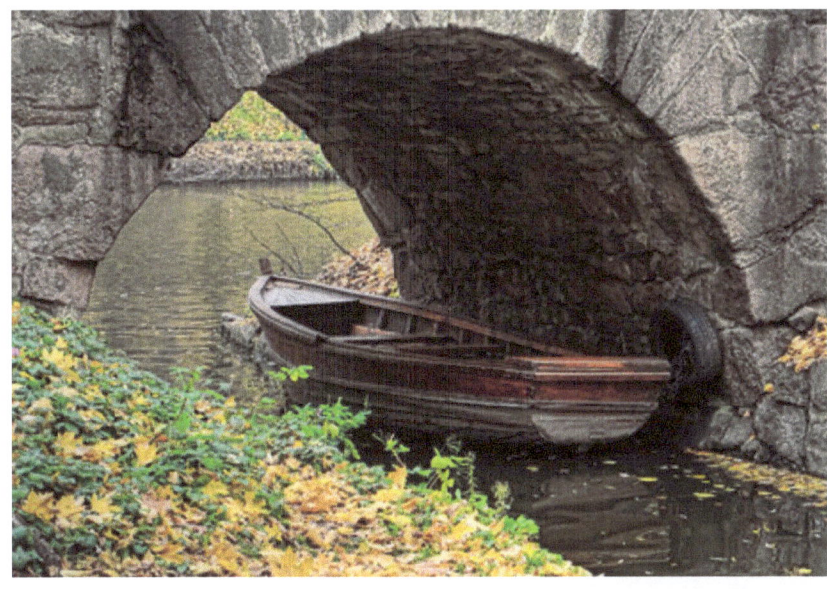

Original Photo

Photoshop CS5, Actions, Panos FX Puzzle, Plug-In

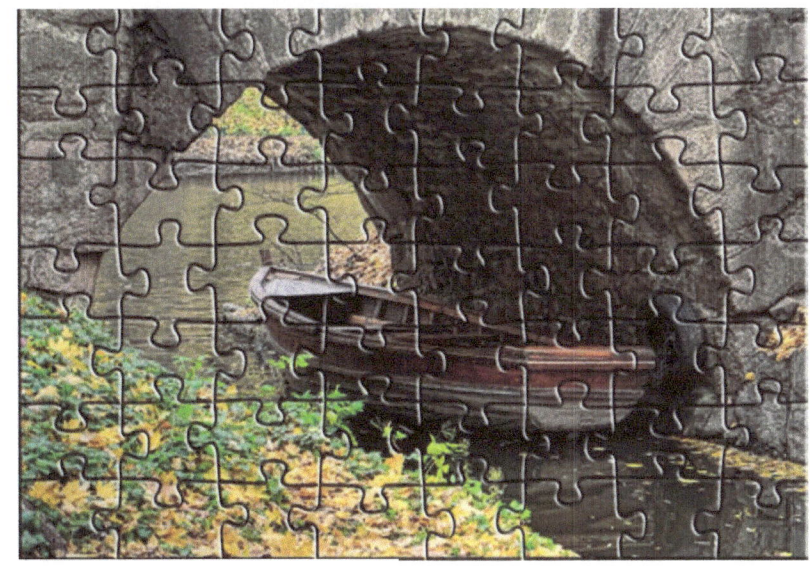

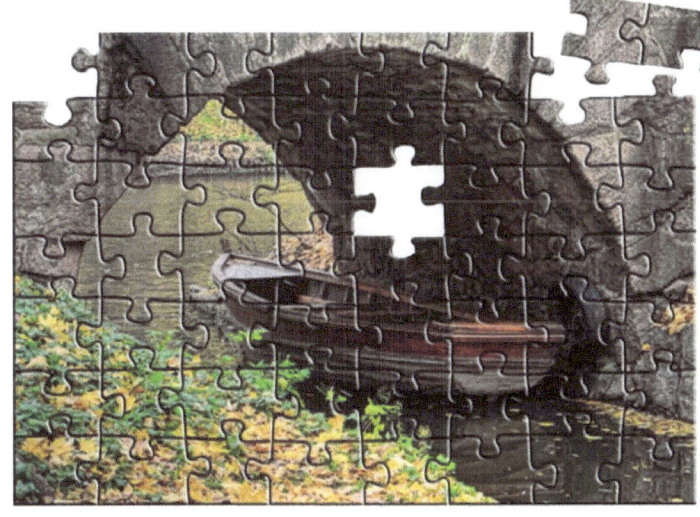

Photoshop CS5, Actions, Panos FX Puzzle, Quick Selection Tool, Edit, Free Transform

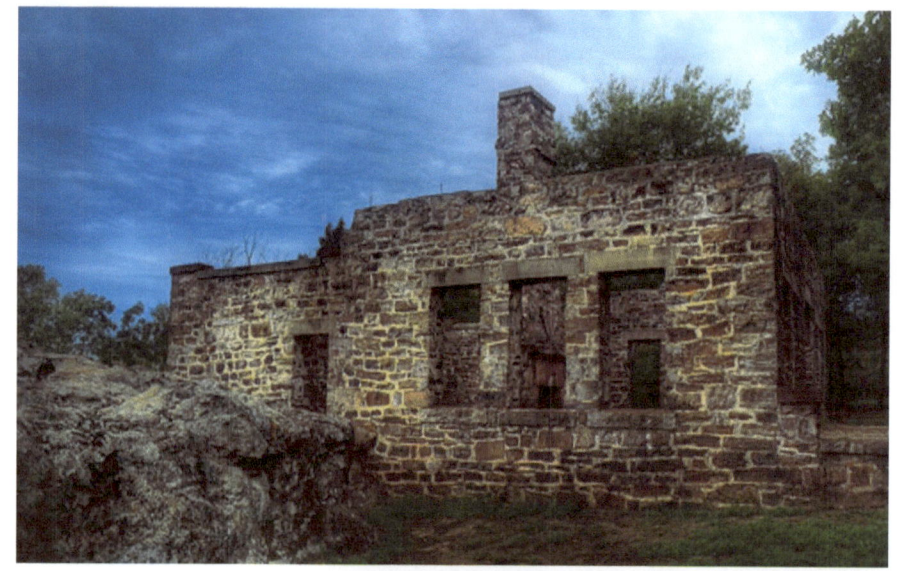

Original Photo

Photoshop CS5, Nik Software, Color Efex Pro 3, Plug-In

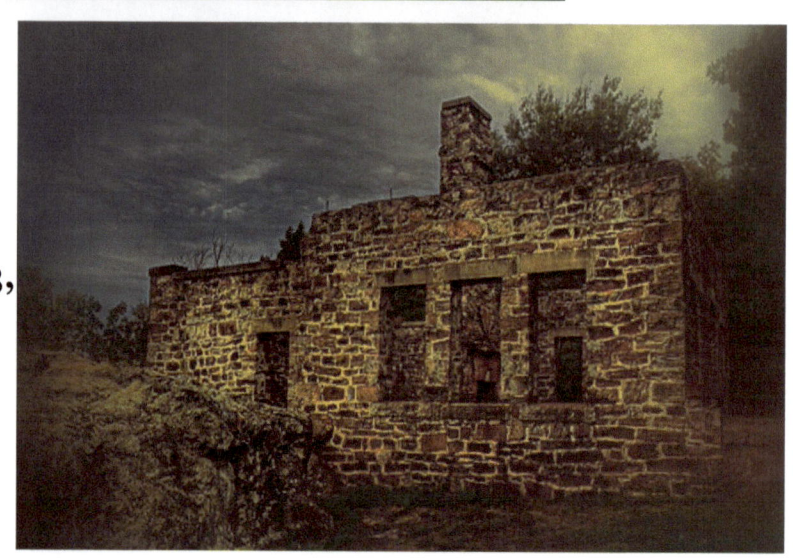

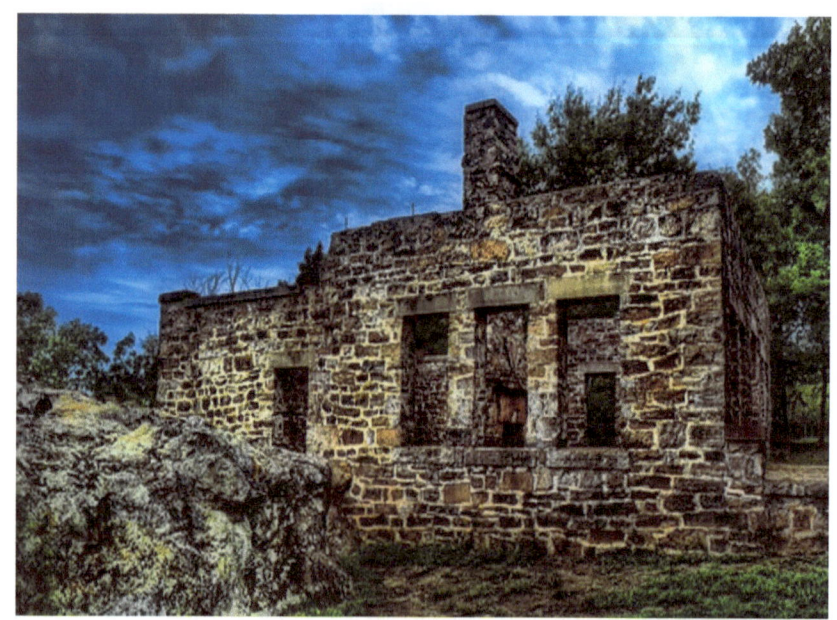

Photoshop CS5, Topaz Labs, Adjust 3, Plug-In

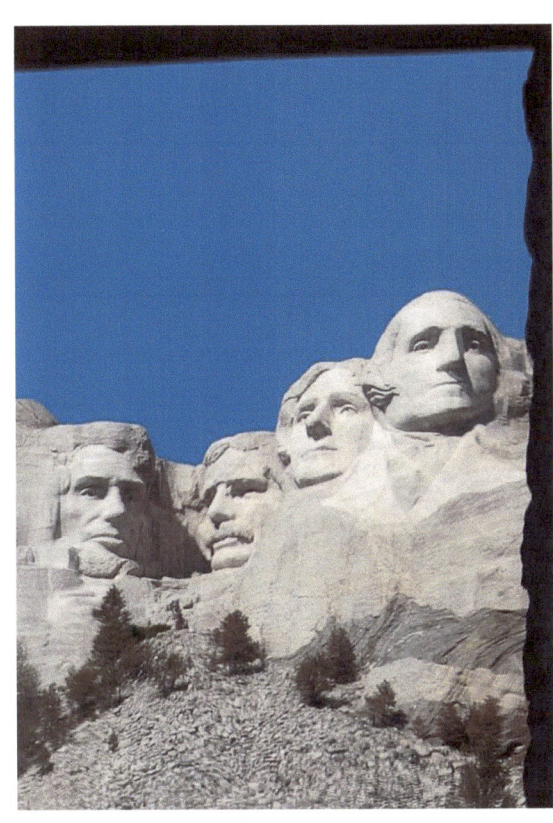

Photoshop CS5, Nik Software, Define 2, onOne Software, Photo Frame 4.5, Plug-In

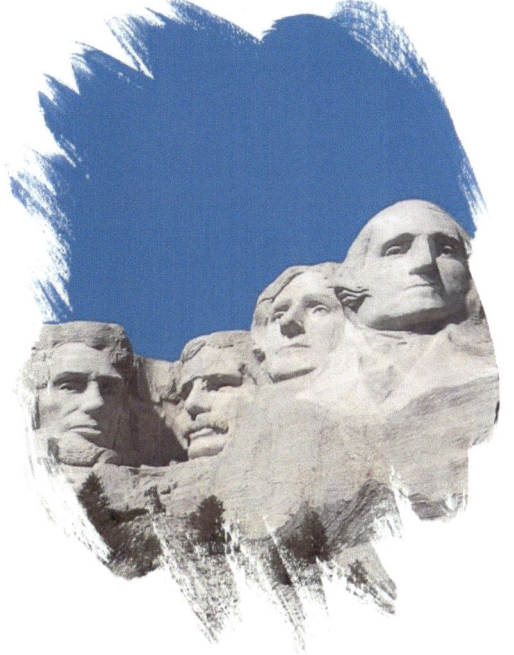

Photoshop CS5, Nik Software, Define 2, onOne Software, Photo Frame 4.5, Plug-In

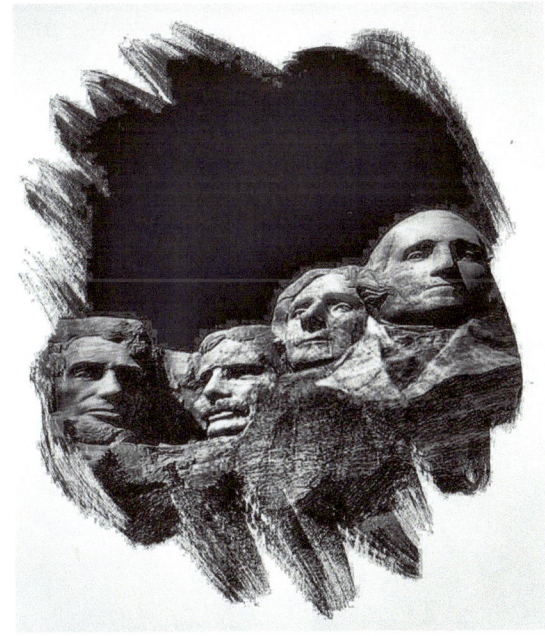

Photoshop CS5, onOne Software, Focal Point 2.5, Photo Frames 4.5, Platinum , Plug-In

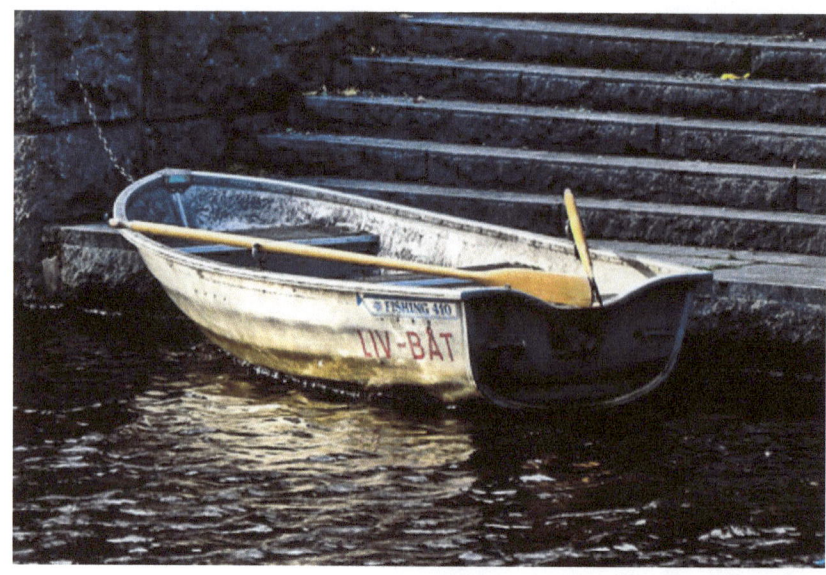

Original Photo

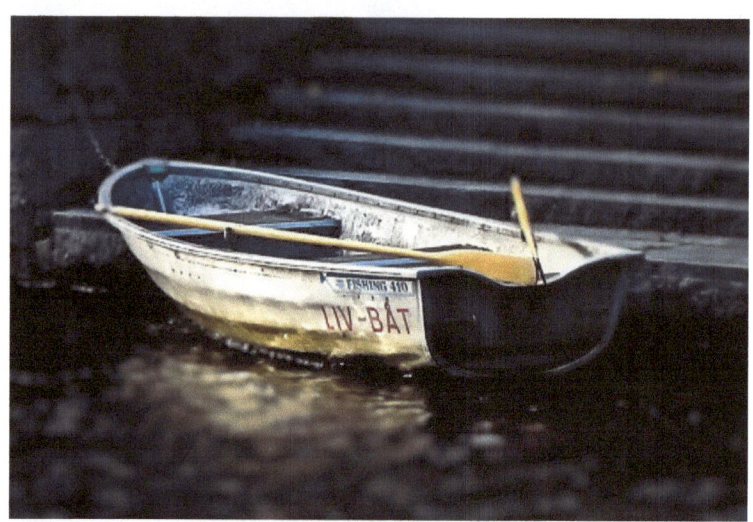

Photoshop CS5, Nik Software, Define 2, Focal Point 2, Plug-In

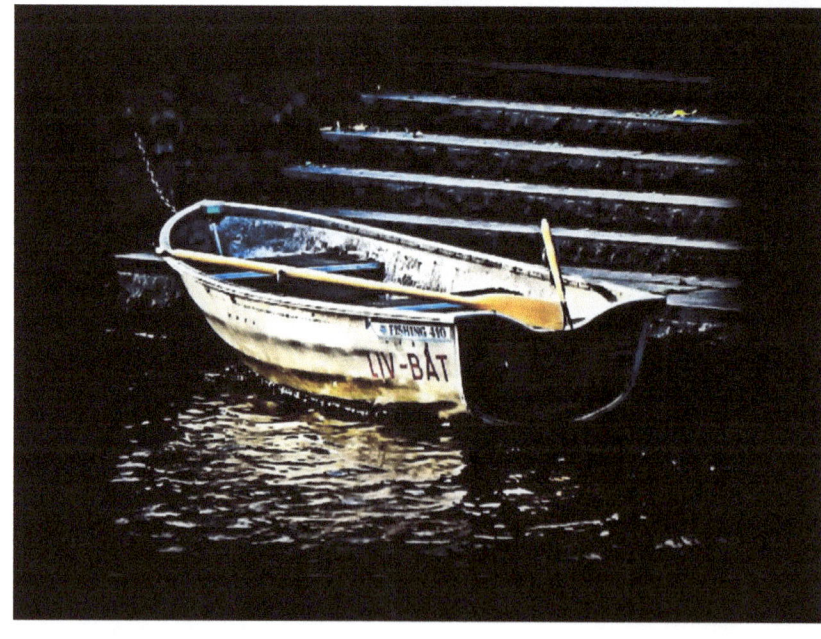

Photoshop CS5, Nik Software Define 2, Photo Tools 2.5, Presets, Plug-In

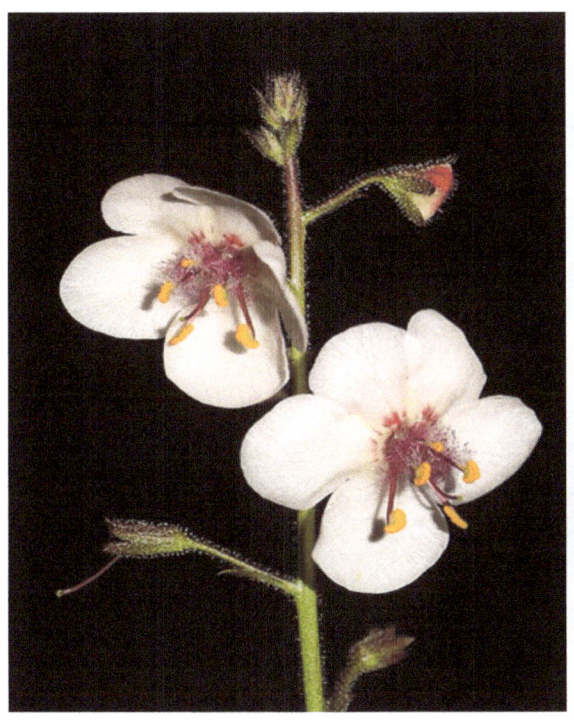

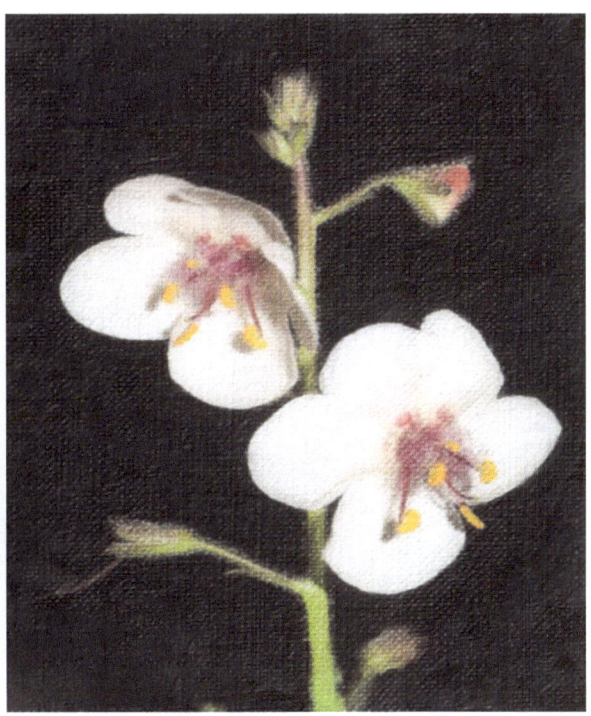

Original Photo

Photoshop CS5, Alien Skin Snap Art, Oil Painting, Plug-In

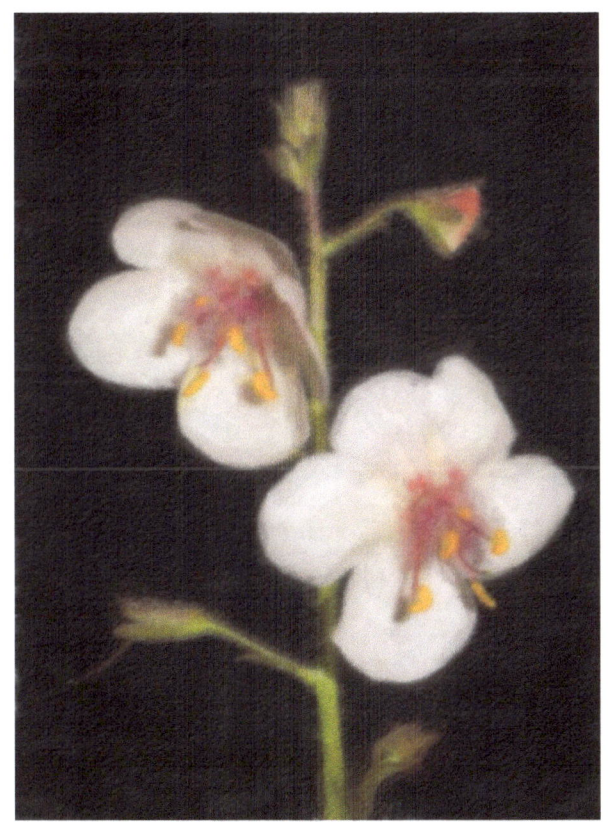

Photoshop CS5, Alien Skin Snap Art, Watercolor, Plug-In

It is hard to see the actual texture of these prints unless they were printed full page.

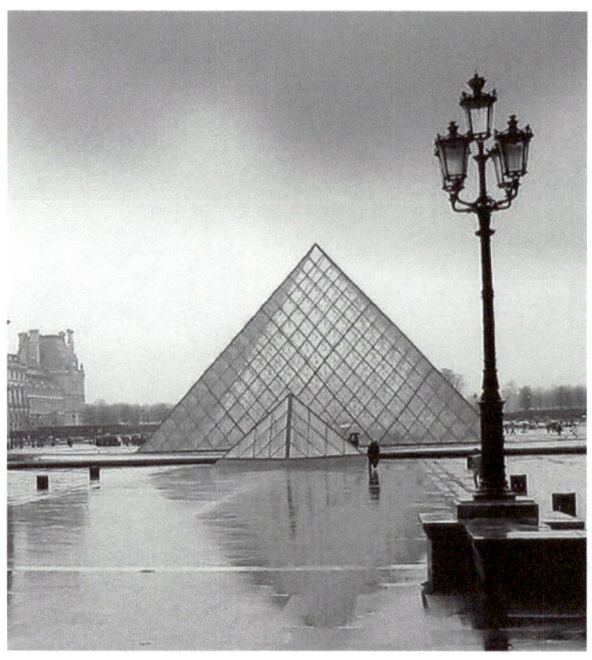

Original Print

Photoshop CS5, Nik Software, Define 2, Sharpener Pro 3.0, onOne Software, Photo Tools 2.5, Presets, Plug-In

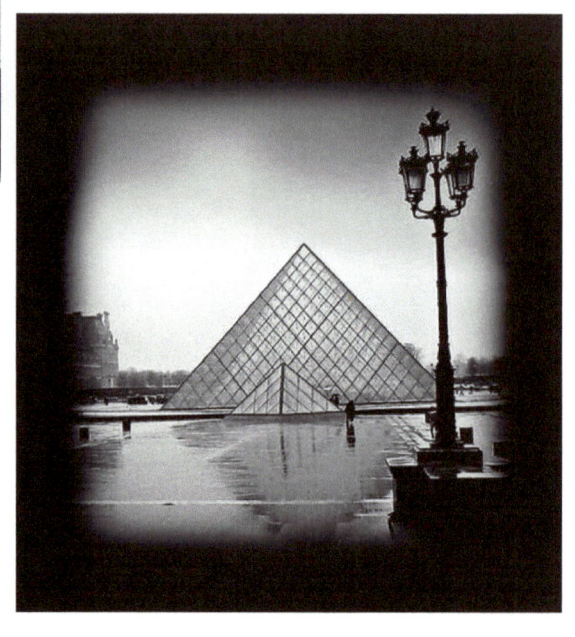

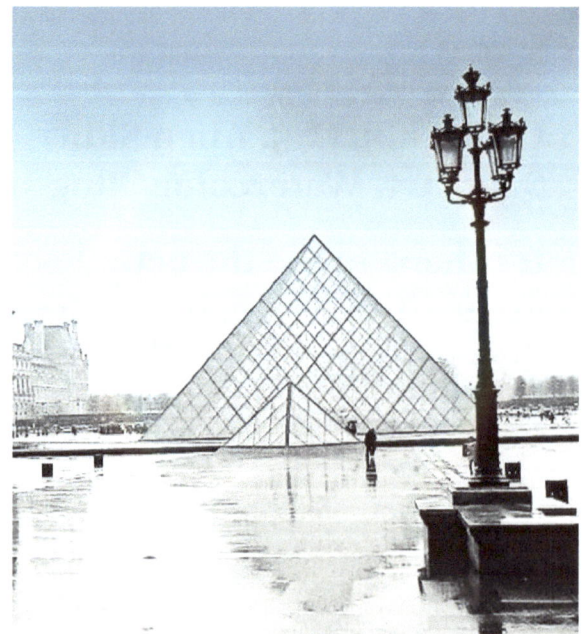

Photoshop CS5, onOne Software, Photo Tools 2.5, Rainbow , Preset, Plug-In

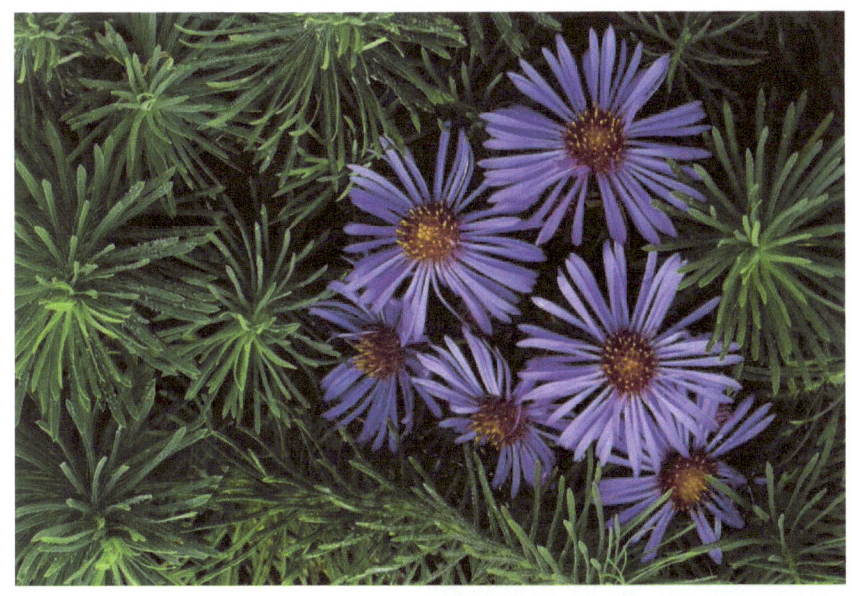

Original Photo

Photoshop CS5, onOne Software, Focal Point 2, Plug-In

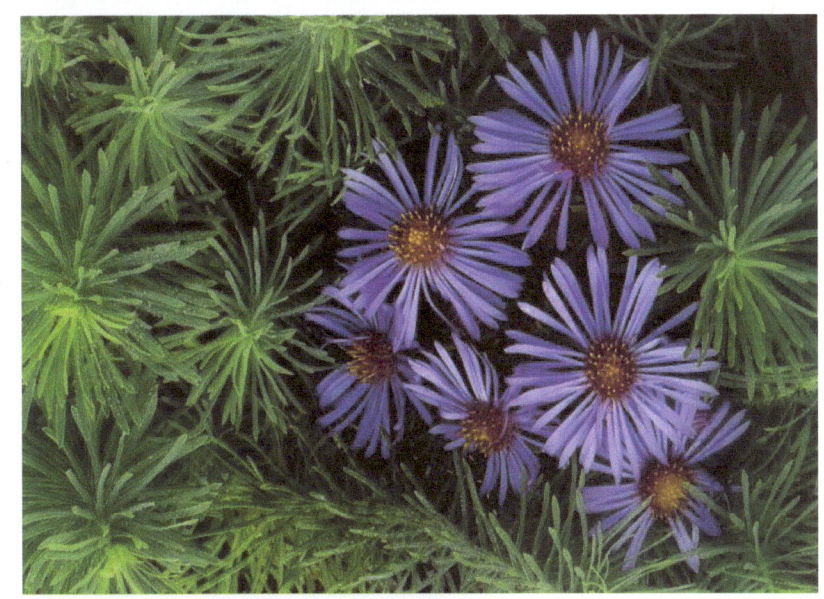

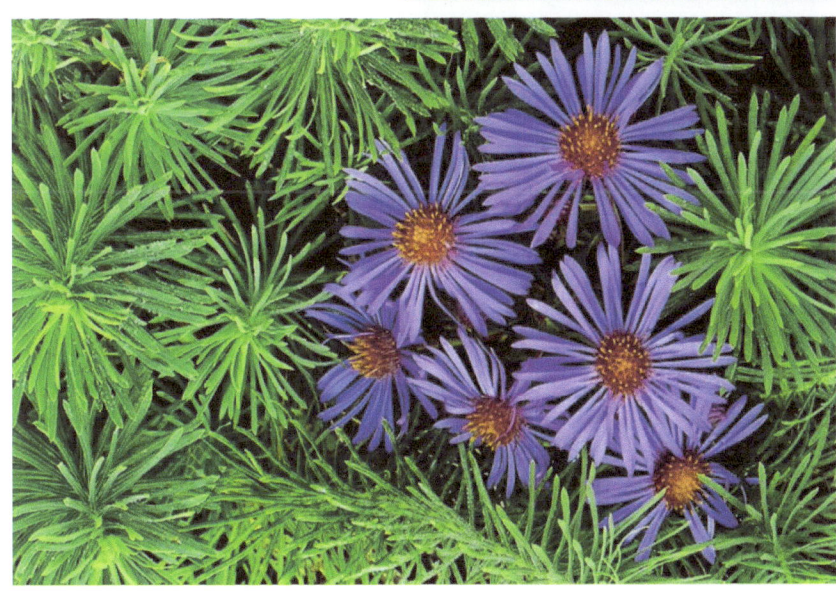

Photoshop CS5, onOne Software, Photo Tune 3, Plug-In

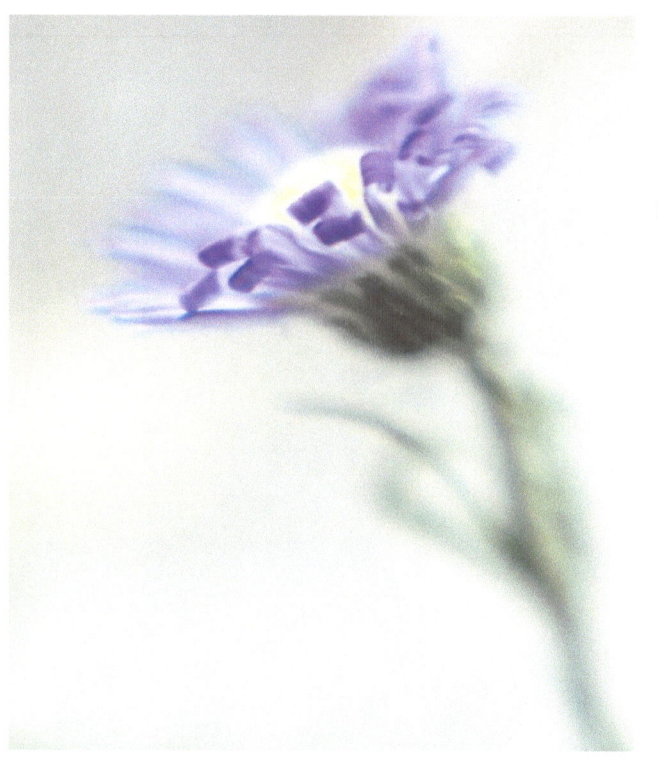

Original Photo

Photoshop CS5, Nik Software, Define 2, Color Efex Pro, Plug-In

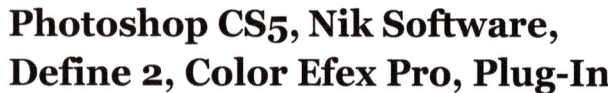

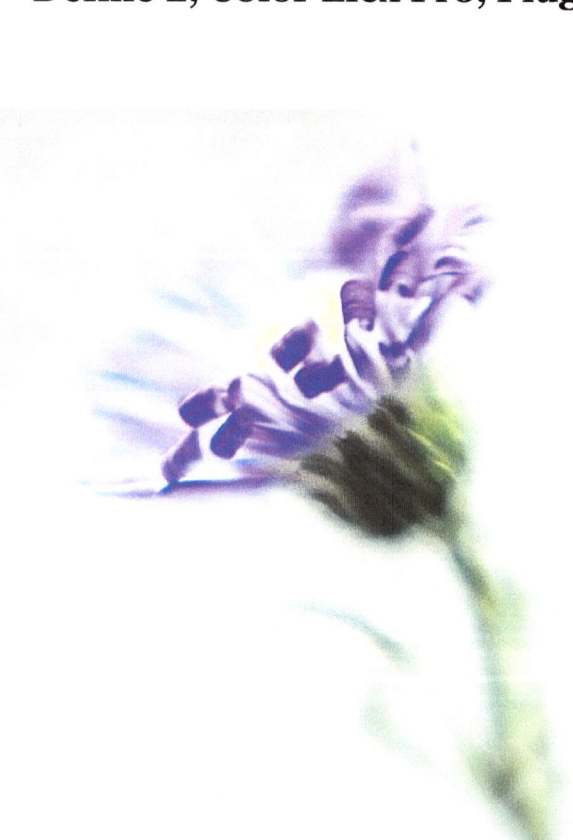

Photoshop CS5, onOne Software, Photo Tools 2.5, Presets, Plug-In

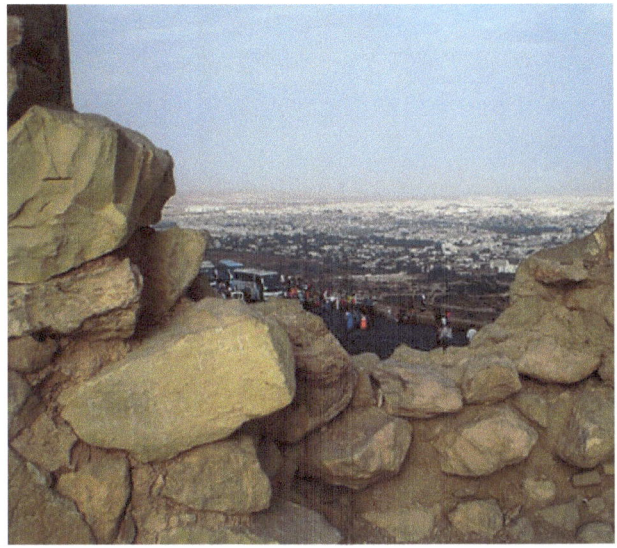

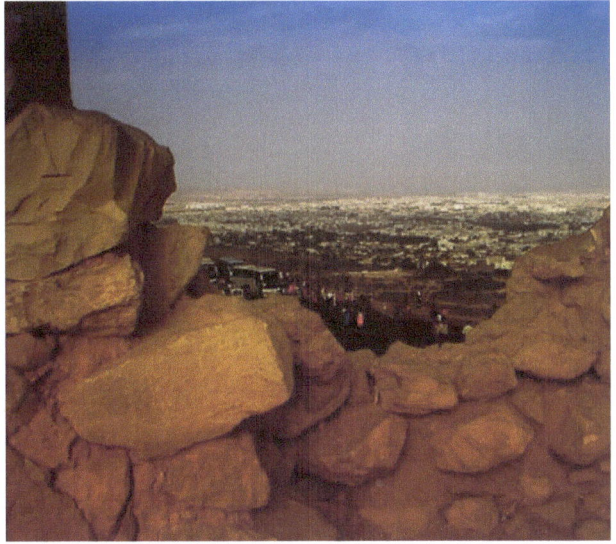

Original Photo

Photoshop CS5, Nik Software,
Define 2, Color Efex Pro 3,
Plug-In

Photoshop CS5, Quick
Selection Tool, to cut out the
foreground of first image and
merge on to second image.

Photoshop CS5, Nik Software
Define 2, Topaz Labs, Adjust 4,
Spicify, Plug-In

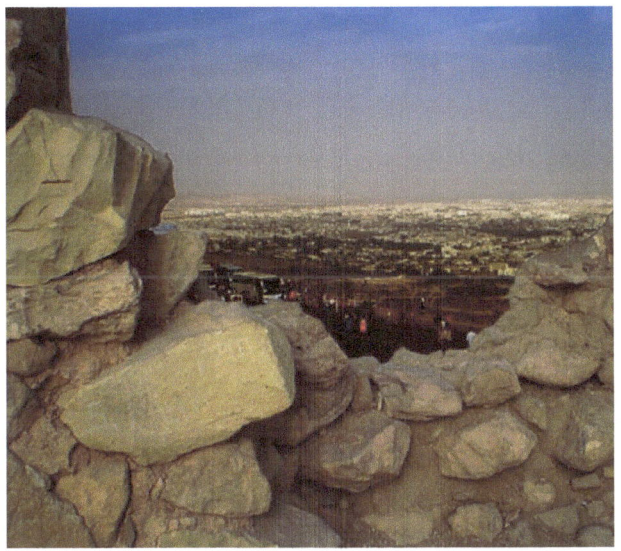

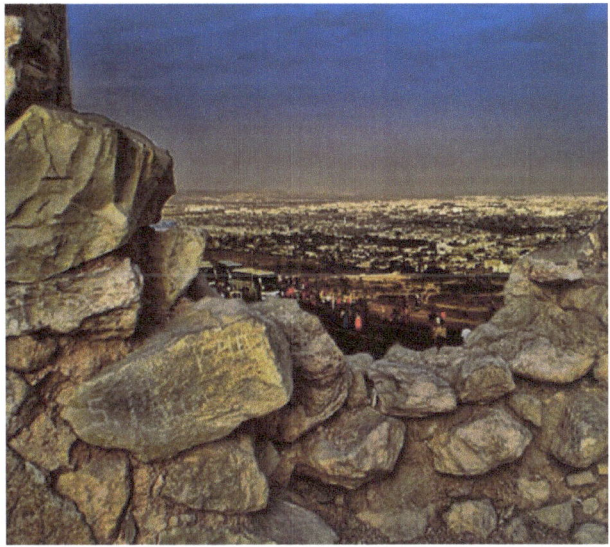

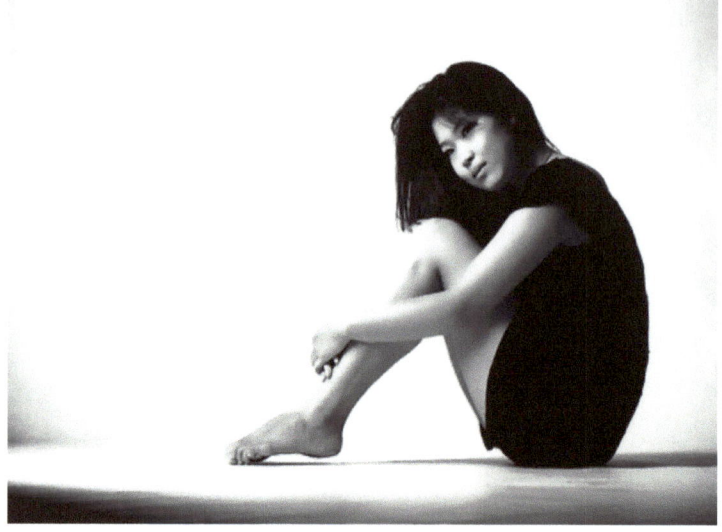

Original Photo

Photoshop CS5, onOne Software, Photo Tools 2.5, Photo Frame 4.5, Plug-In

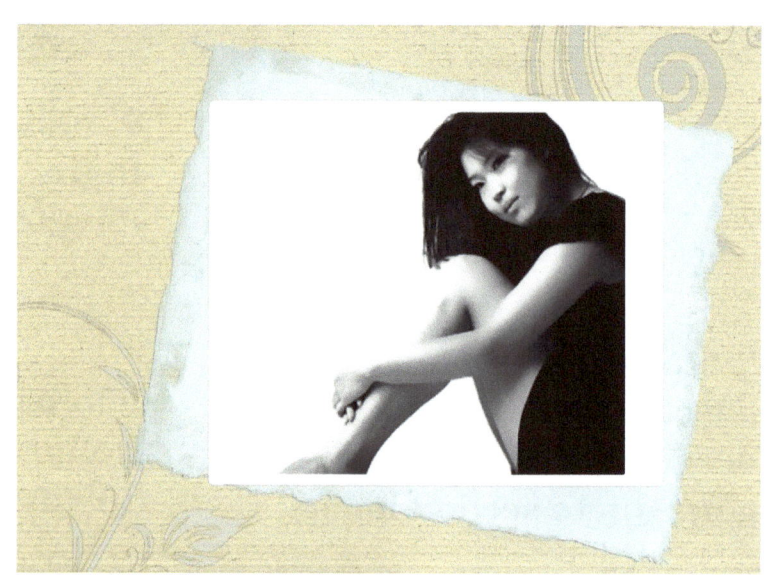

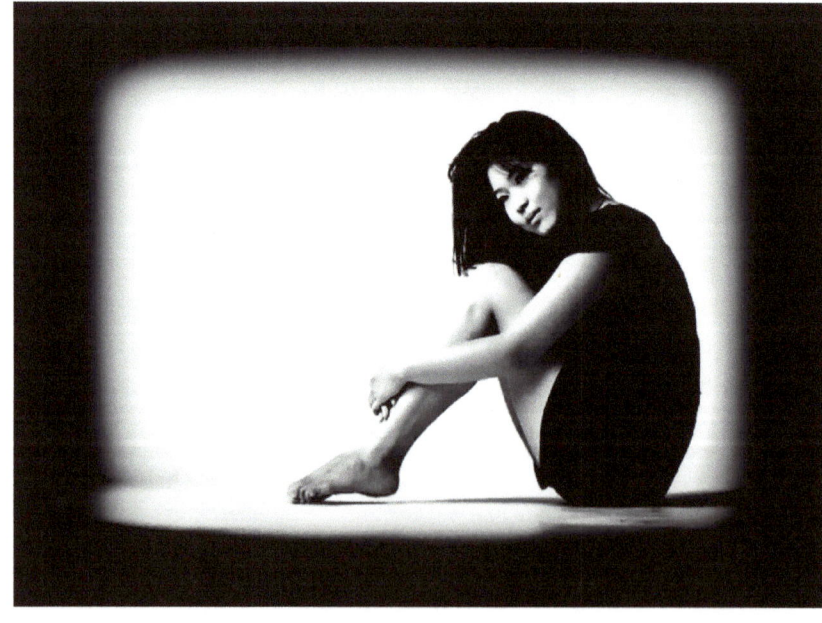

Photoshop CS5, onOne Software, Photo Tools 2.5, Plug-In

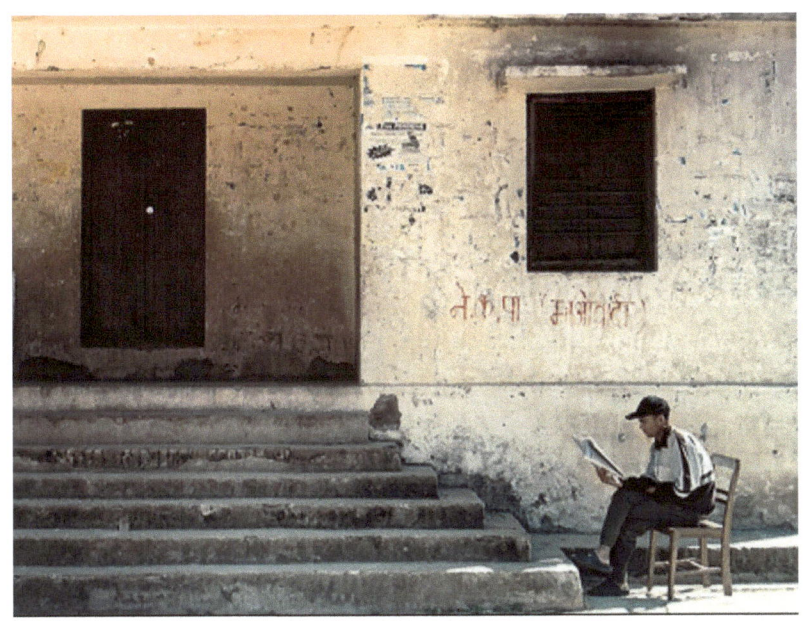

Original Photo

Photoshop CS5, Nik Software, Define 2, Color Efex Pro 3, onOne Software Photo Tools 2.5, Plug-In

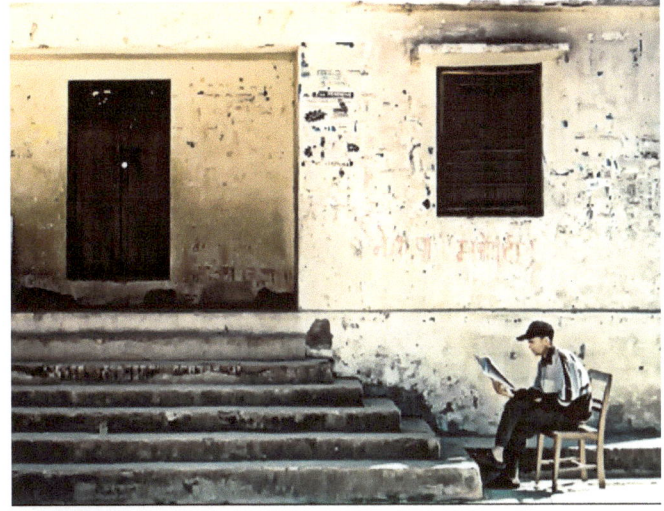

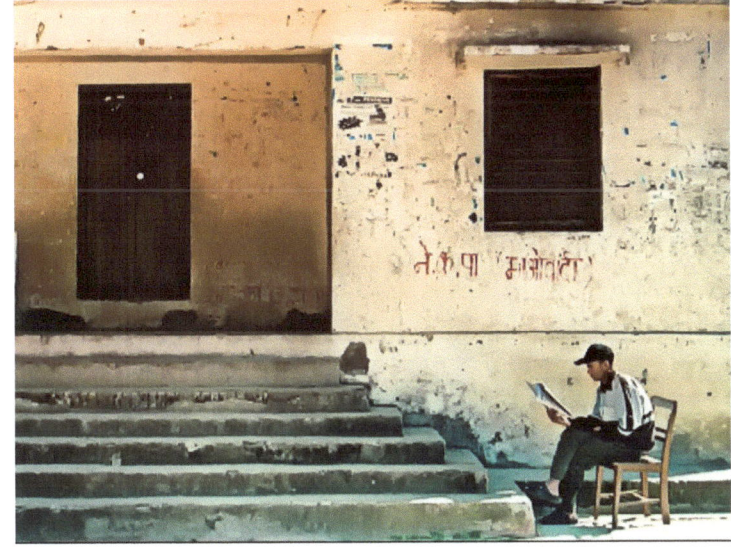

Photoshop CS5, Nik Software Define 2, Color Efex Pro 3, onOne Software, Photo Tools 2.5, Plug-In

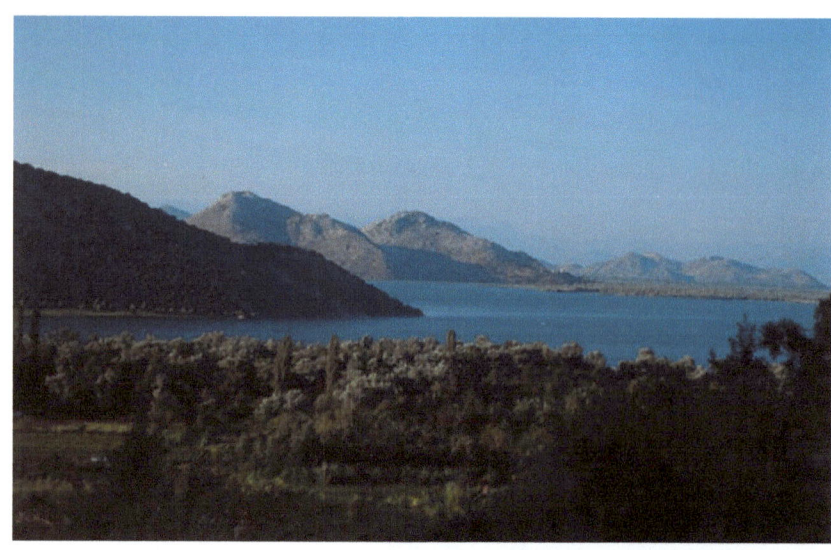

Original Photo

Photoshop CS5, Topaz Labs, DeNoise 5, Adjust 4, Simplify, Plug-In

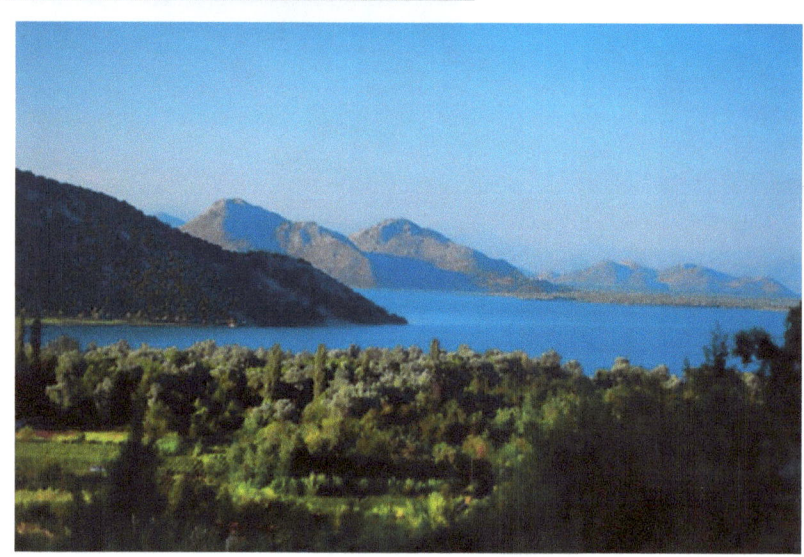

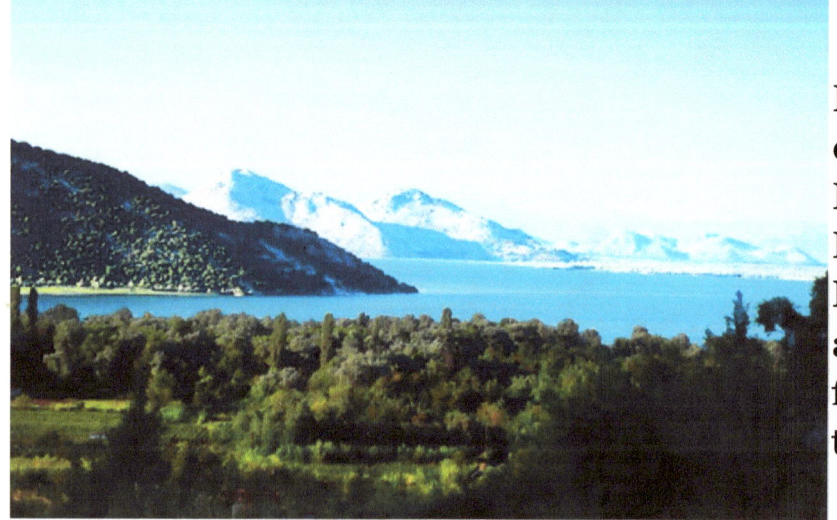

Photoshop CS5, onOne Software, Photo Tools 2.5, Photo Tune 3, Plug-In, then cut and paste the foreground from the image above.

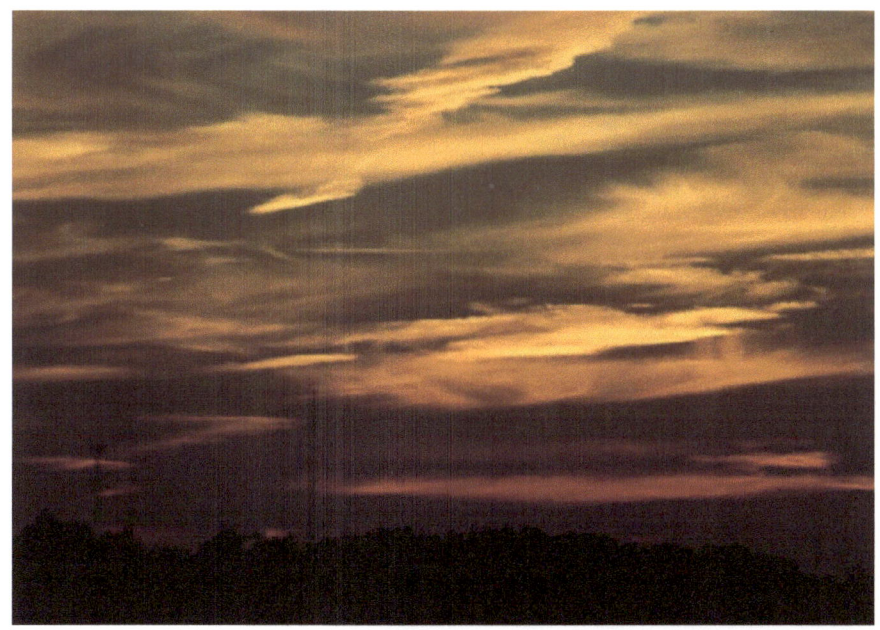

Original Photo

Photoshop CS5, onOne Software Photo Tools 2.5, Topaz Labs Adjust 4, Plug-Ins

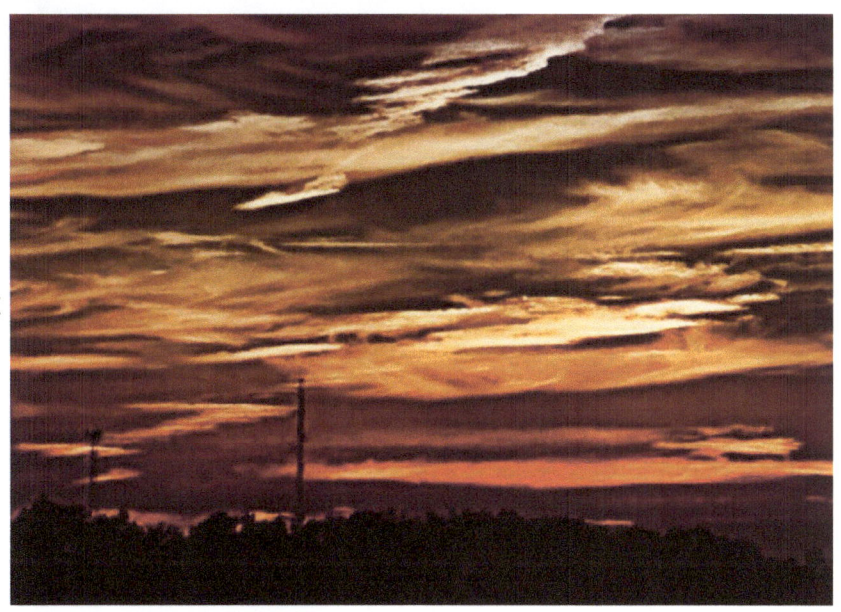

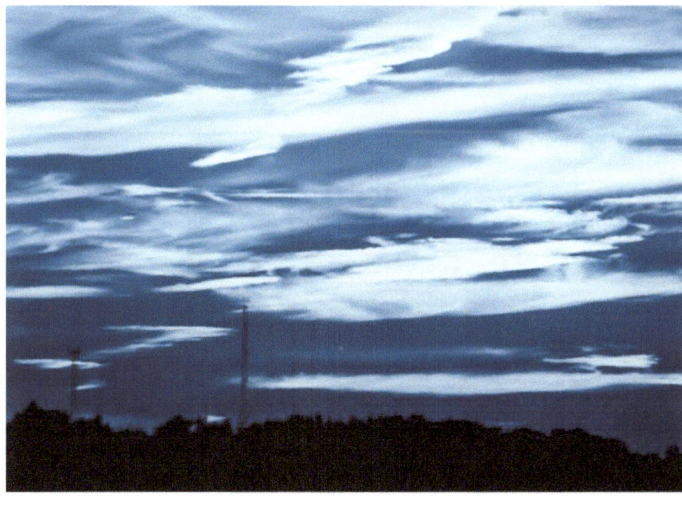

Photoshop CS5, Nik Software Silver Efex Pro, Plug-In

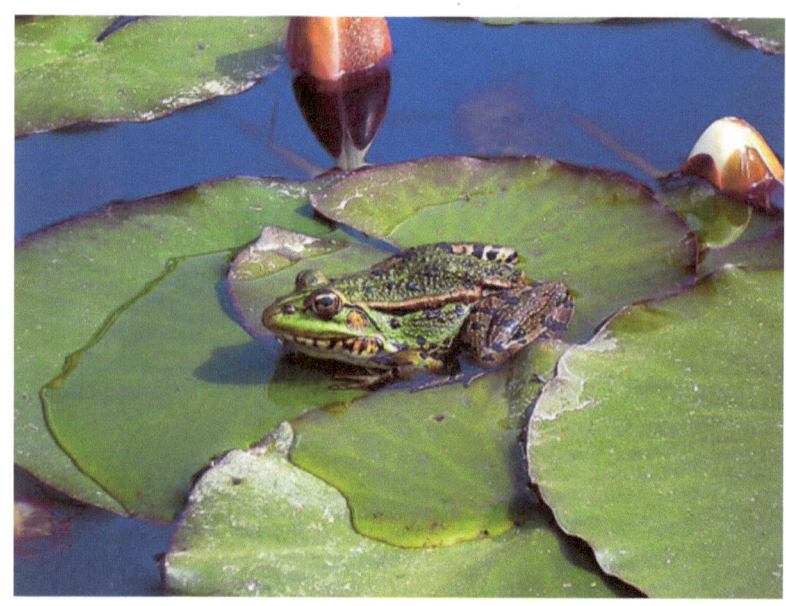

Original Photo

**Photoshop CS5,
onOne Software,
Focal Point 2, Plug-In**

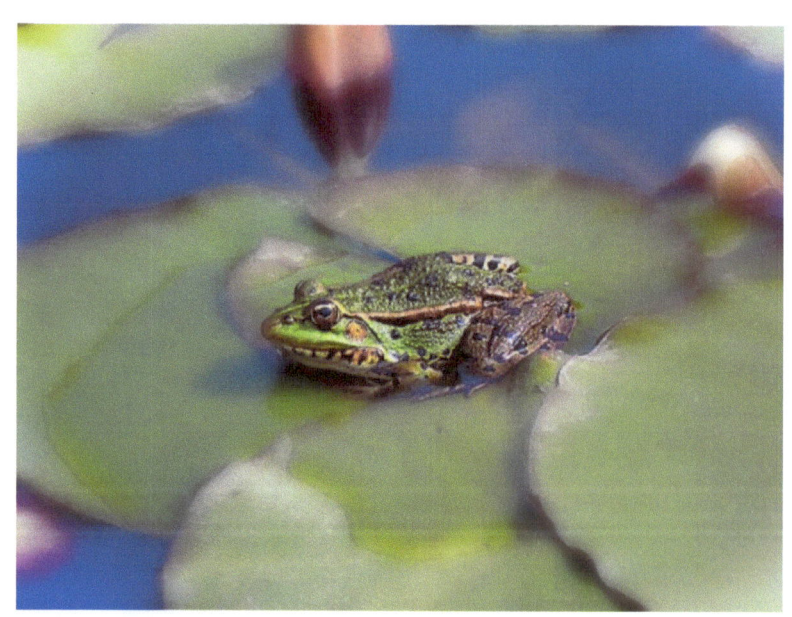

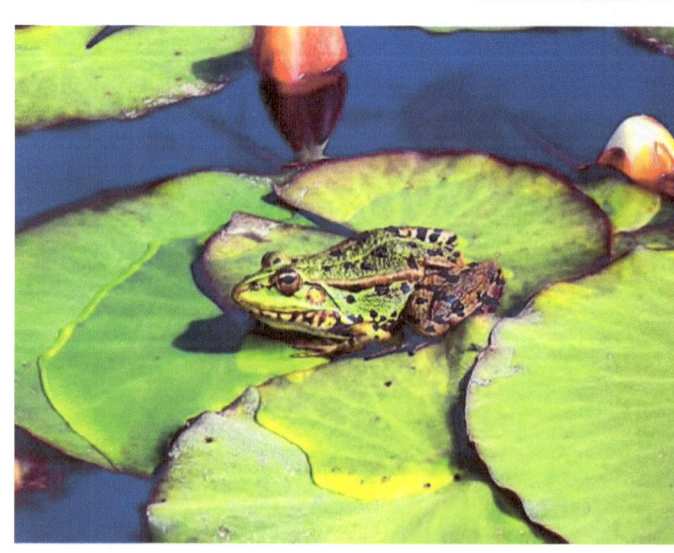

**Photoshop CS5, Topaz
Labs, Detail 2, DeNoise
5, Plug-In**

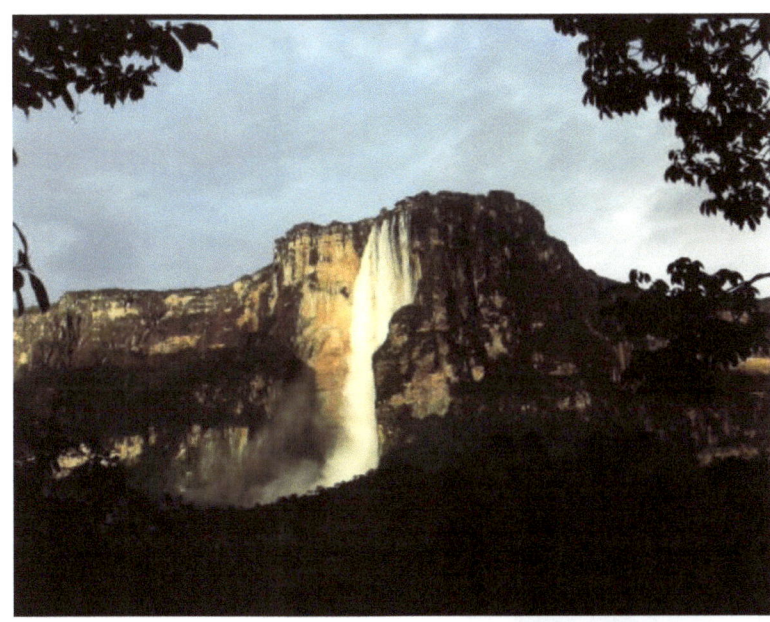

Original Photo

Photoshop CS5, Topaz deNoise 5, Nik Labs, Color Efex Pro 3, Plug-In

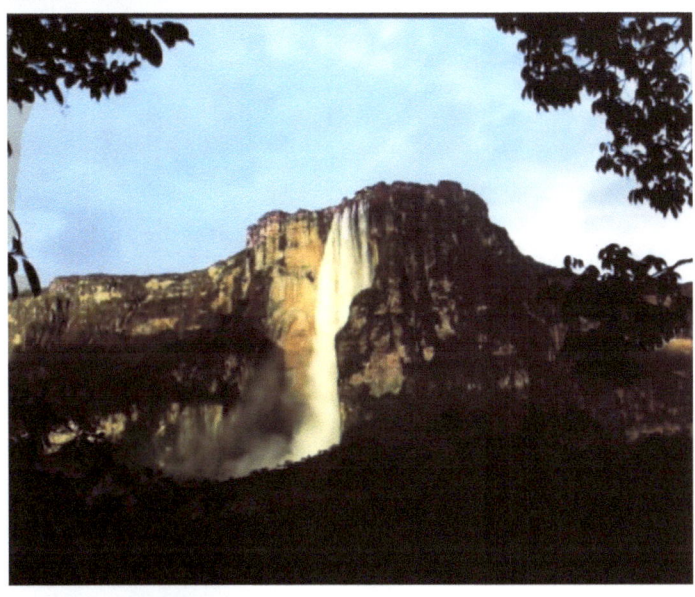

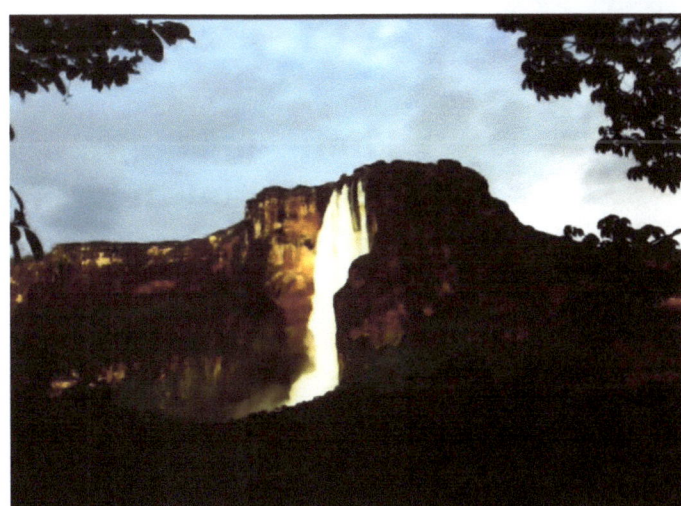

Photoshop CS5, Topaz Software deNoise 5, Detail 2, Plug-In

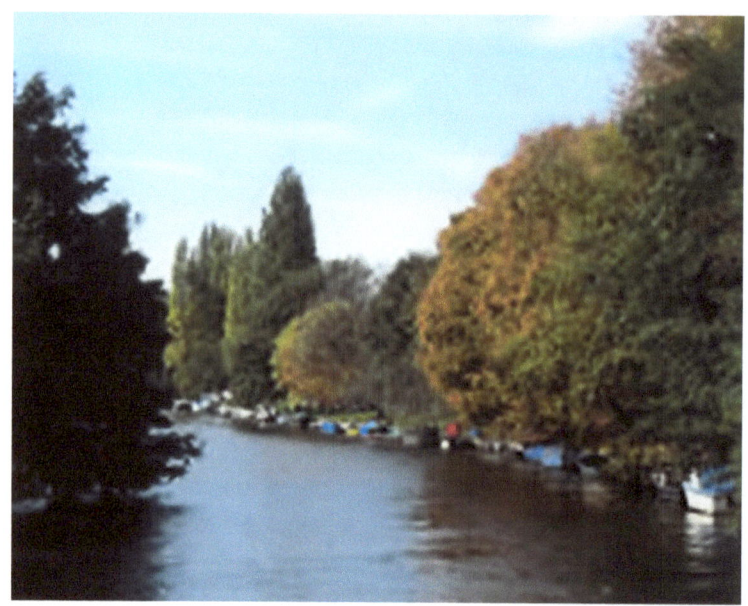

Original Photo

Photoshop CS5, Nik Software Color Efex Pro 3, Plug-In

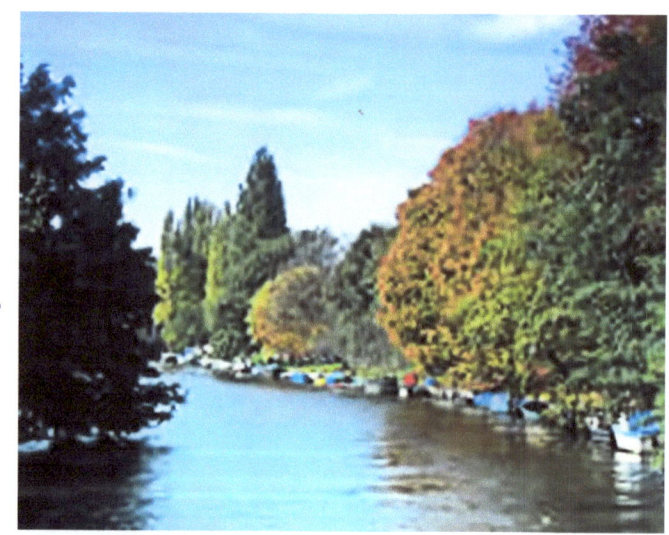

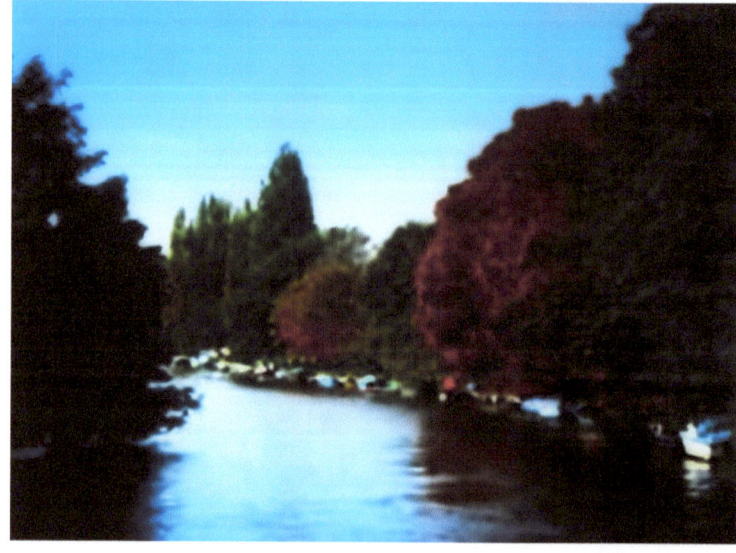

Photoshop CS5, Topaz Detail 2, onOne Software Photo Tools 2.5, Plug-In

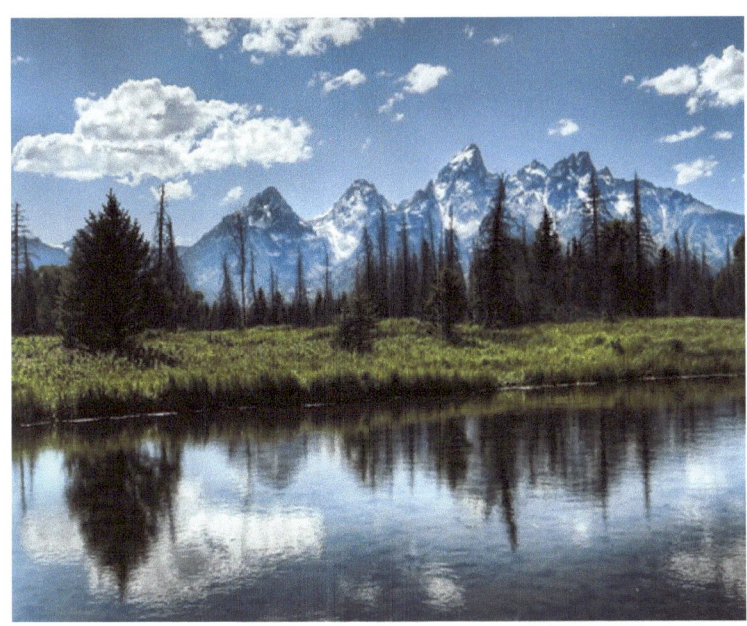

Original Photo

Photoshop CS5, Nik Software Define 2, Silver Efex Pro, Plug-In

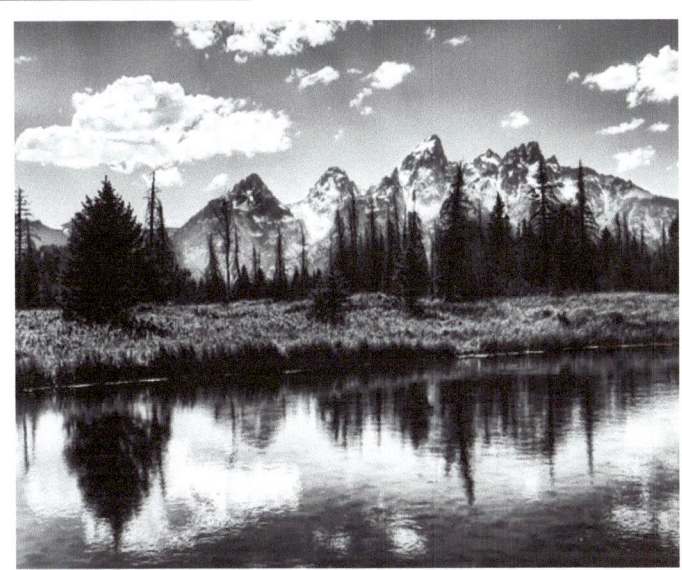

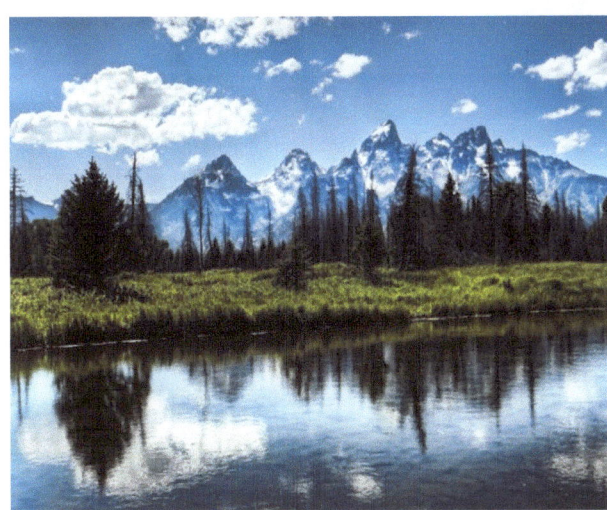

Photoshop CS5, Nik Software Define 2, onOne Software Photo Tools 2.5, Plub-In

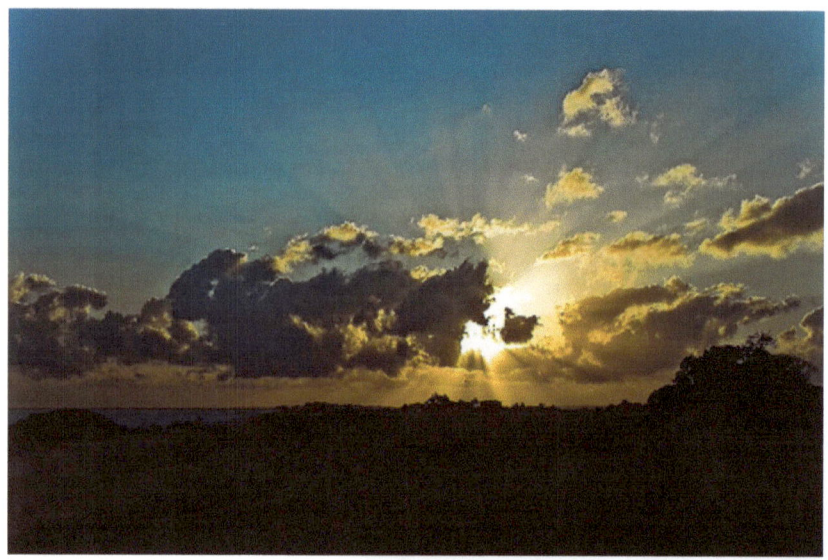

Original Photo

**Photoshop CS5,
Nik Software
Define 2, onOne
Software Photo
Tools 2.5, Plug-In**

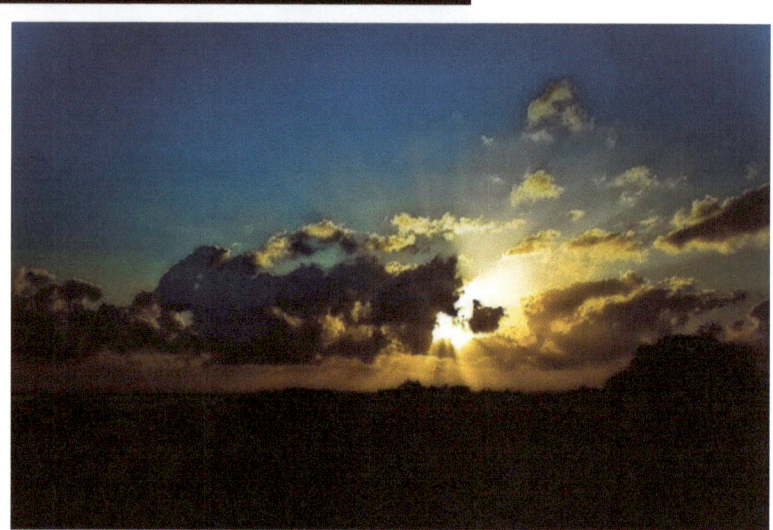

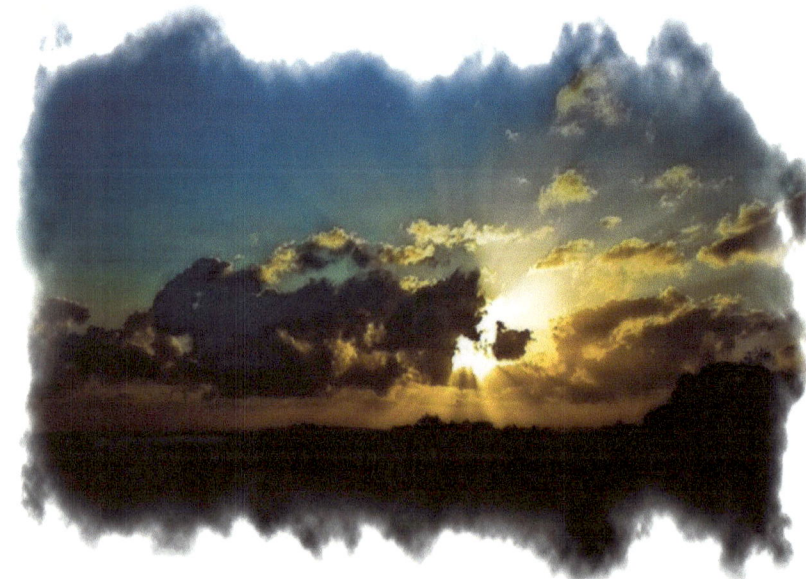

**Photoshop CS5,
onOne Software
Photo Tools 2.5,
Photo Frame 4.5,
Plug-In**

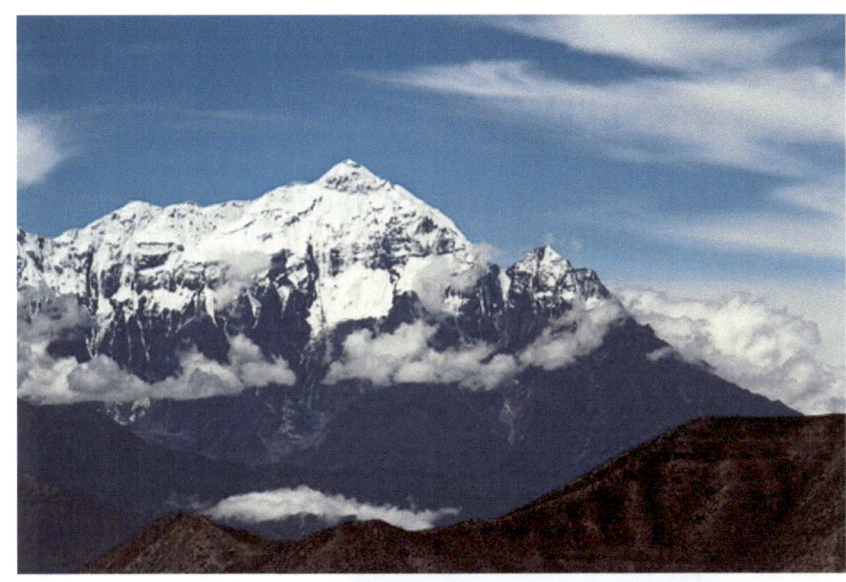

Original Photo

Photoshop CS5, Topaz Adjust Detail 2 Deep Blue, Plug--In

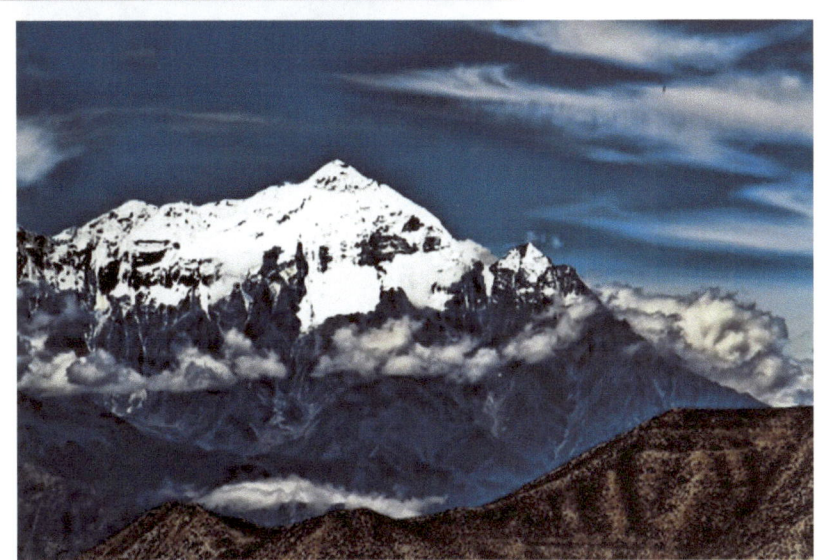

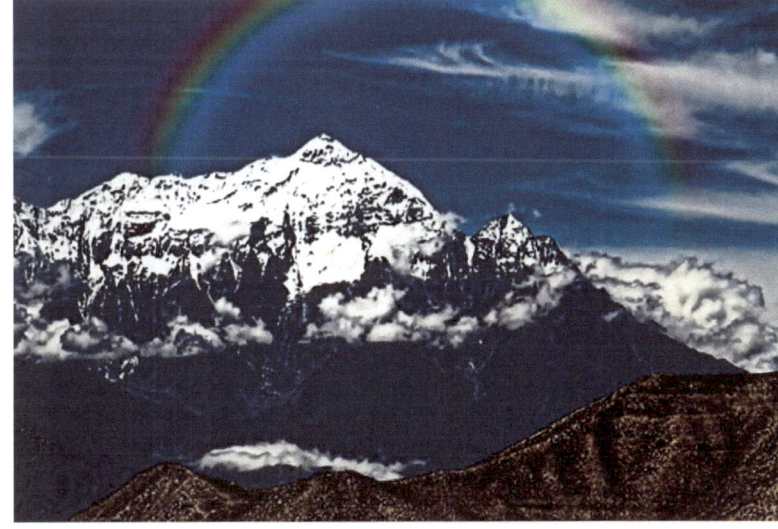

Photoshop CS5, Photo Tools 2.5 Landscape, Rainbow, Plug-In

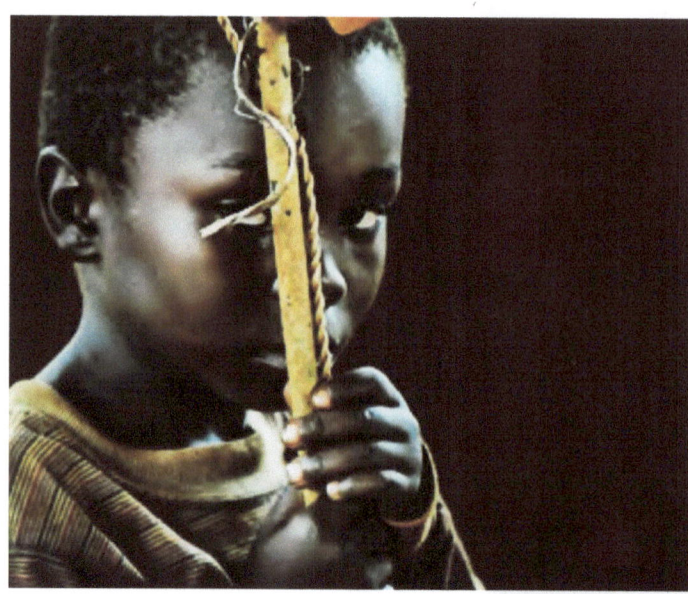

Original Photo

Photoshop CS5, onOne Software, Color Tools 2.5, Presets, Plug-In

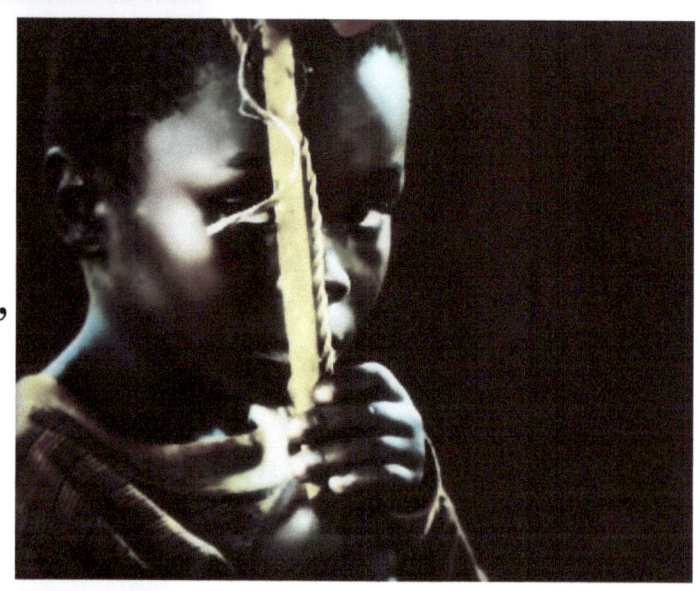

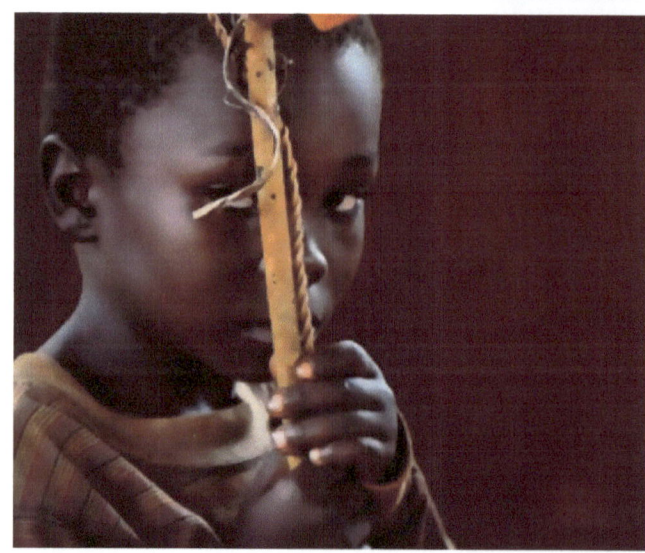

Photoshop CS5, Topaz Labs, Detail 2, Plug-In

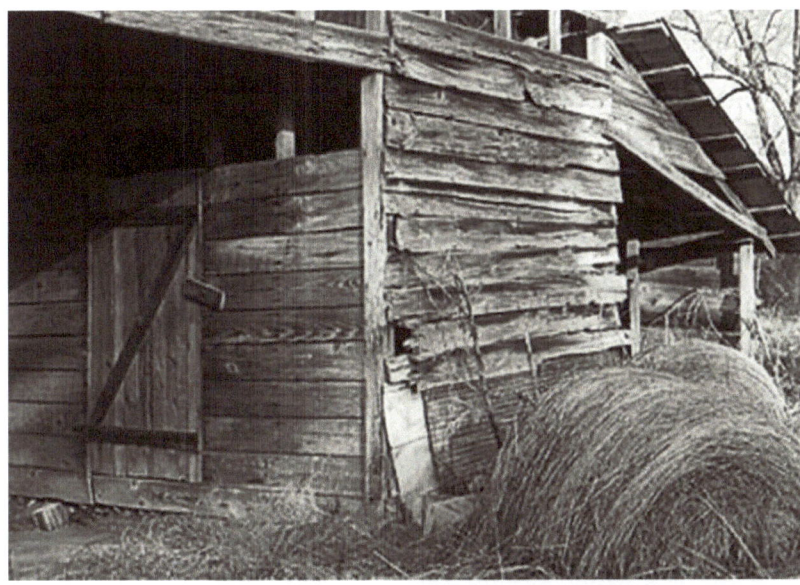

Original Photo

Photoshop CS5 Nik Software Define 2, Color Efex Pro 3, Plug-In

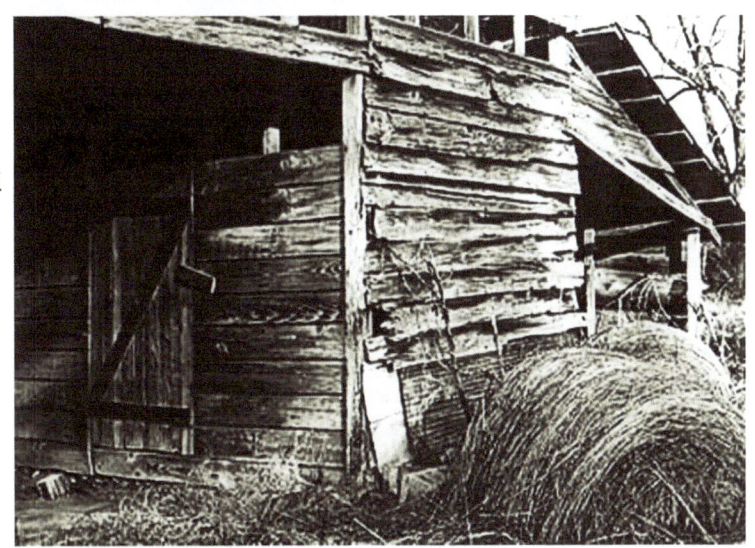

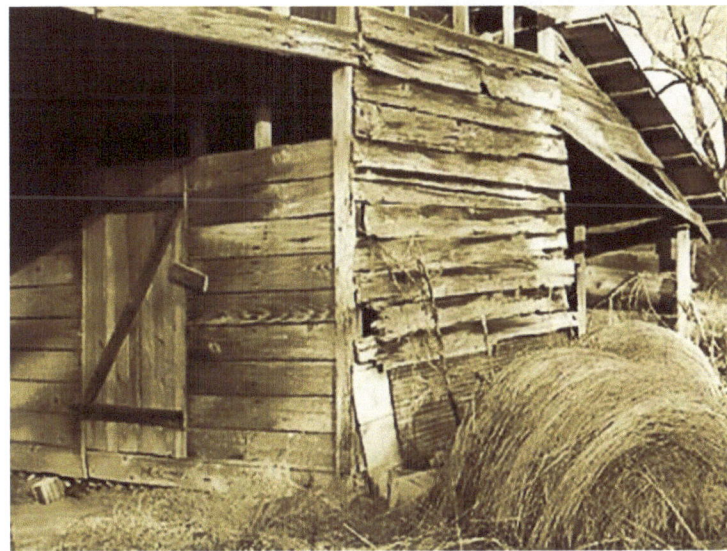

Photoshop CS5 onOne Software, Photo Tools 2.5. Landscape, Plug-In

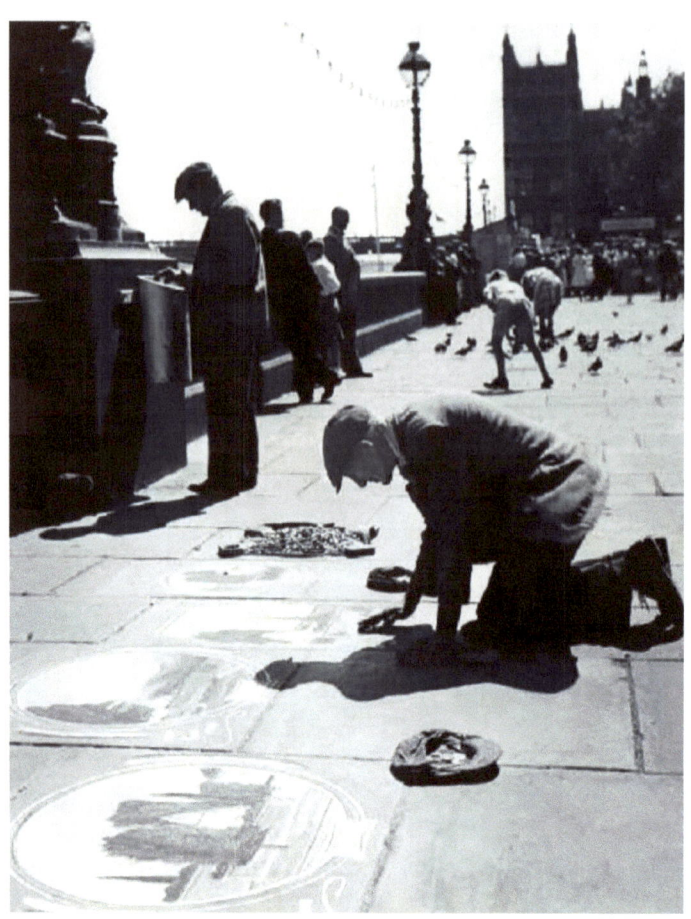

Original Photo from 1958

Photoshop CS5, onOne
Software Photo Tools 2.5

After the B&W photo was
converted to a color print it
still showed the chalk
drawings slightly washed out.
To show what the artist's
work looked like originally, I
cut and pasted a color print
over one of the chalk
drawings.

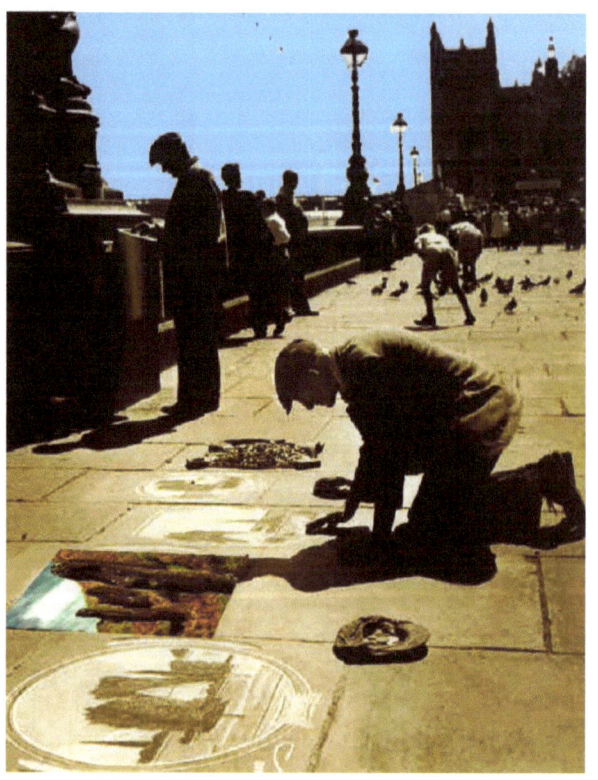

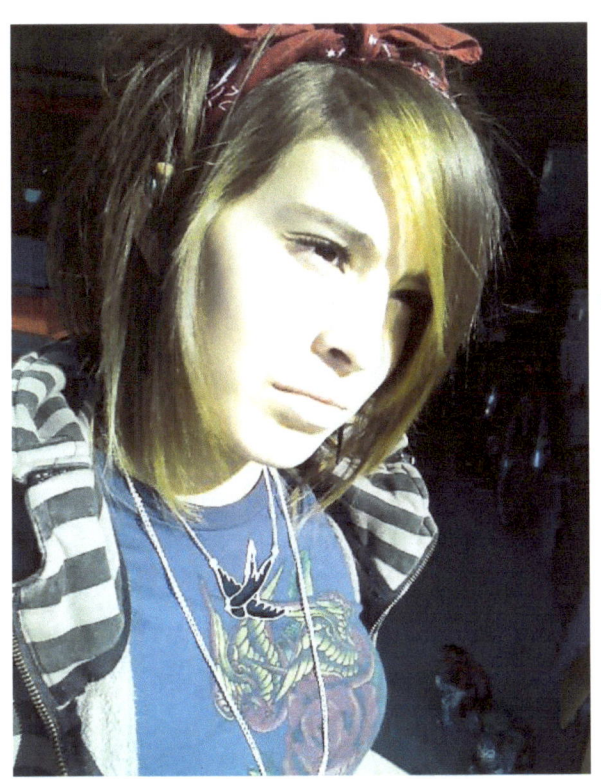

Original Photo

Photoshop CS5, onOne Software, Photo Frame 5, Plug–In

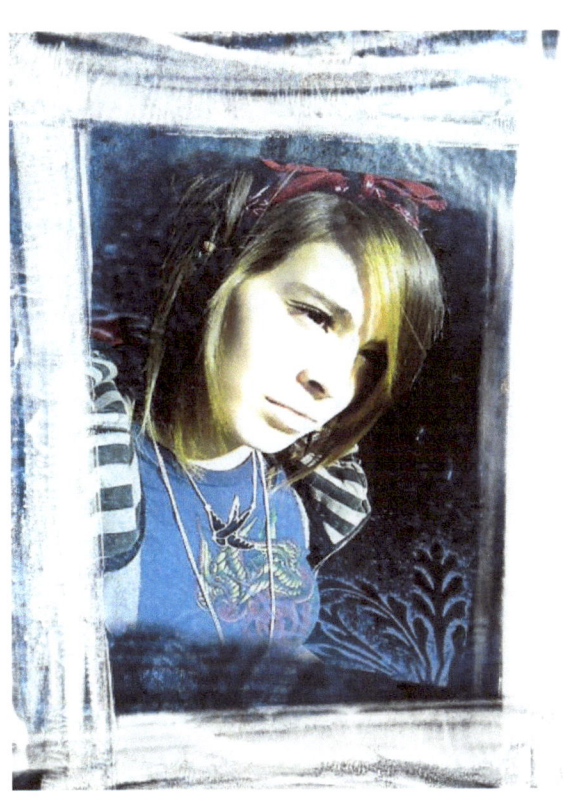

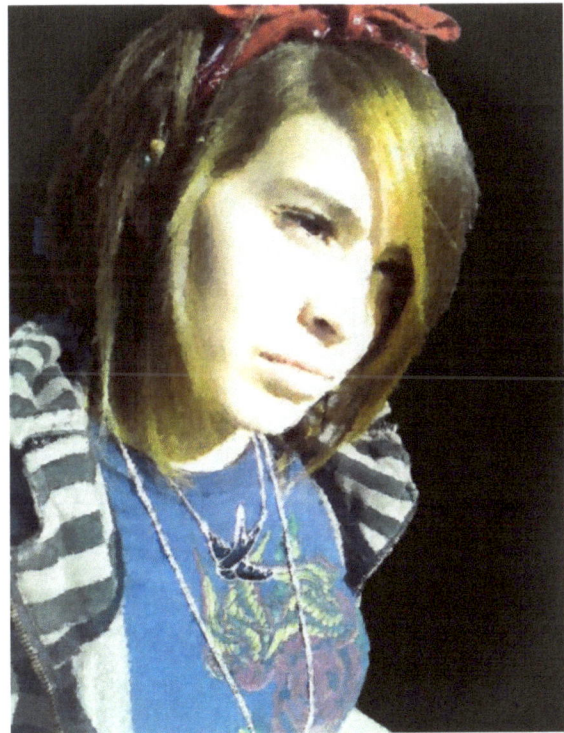

Photoshop CS5, Ailen Skin Software, Snap Art Impasto, Plug-In

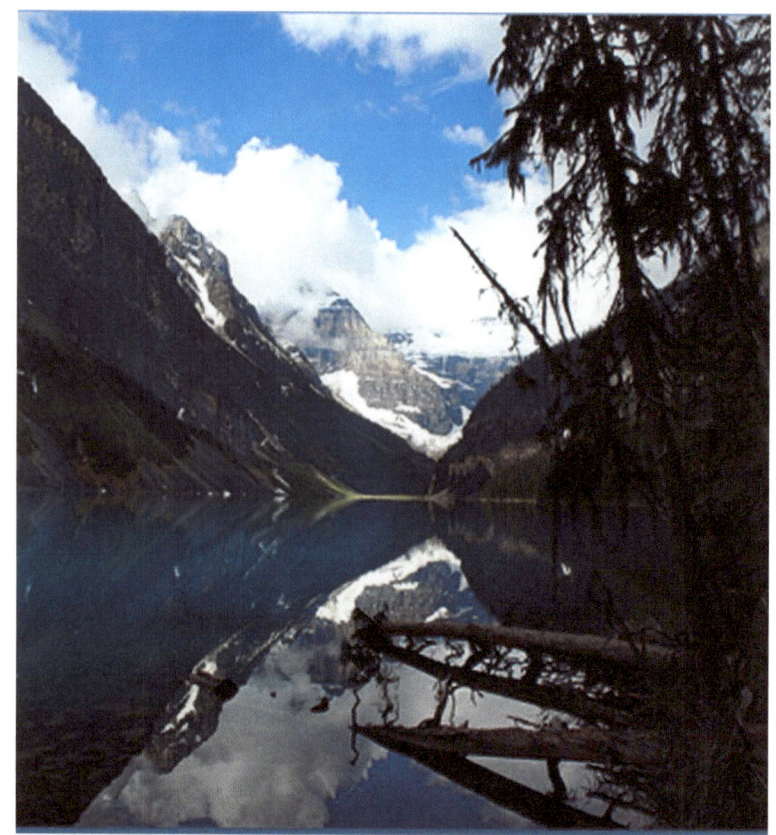

Original Photo

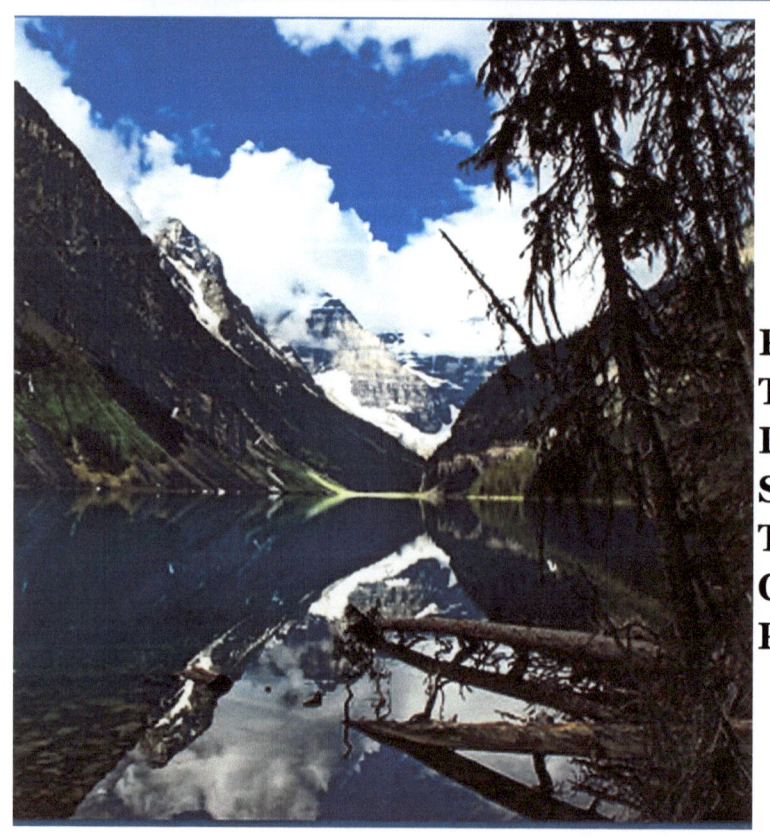

Photoshop CS5, Topaz Labs Detail 2 Deep Blue, onOne Software Photo Tools 2, Landscape Global Sharpening, Plug-In

onOne Software's Mask Pro 4.1 Plug-In offers one of the best ways to cut an image from a photo and then paste it on to another image. It offers the simplicity of cutting out the finest details like you see in the photos below. Notice how the thinnest strands of hair have been removed from the original print.

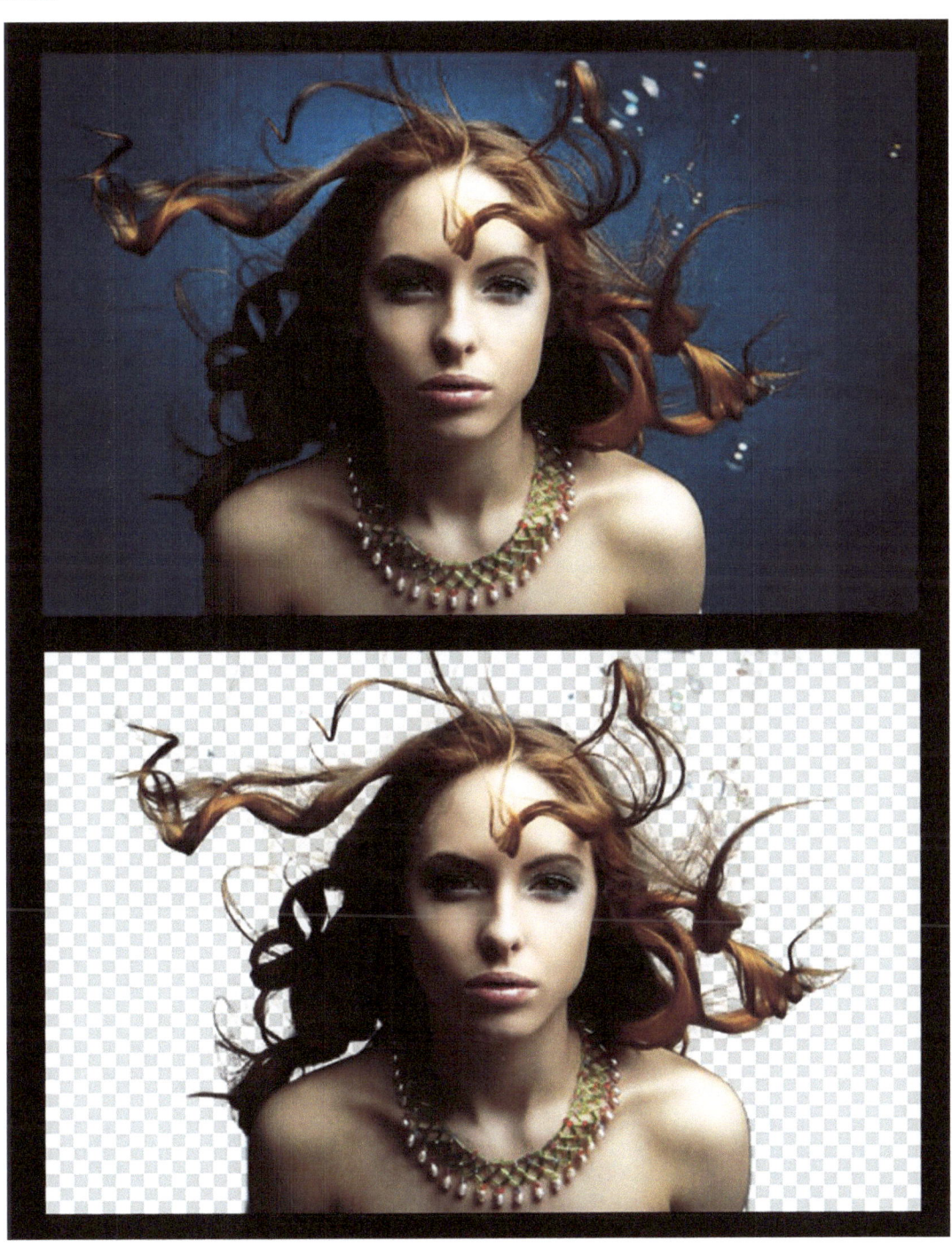

onOne Software, Mask Pro 4.1 Plug-In, image is ready to move and paste on to another image.

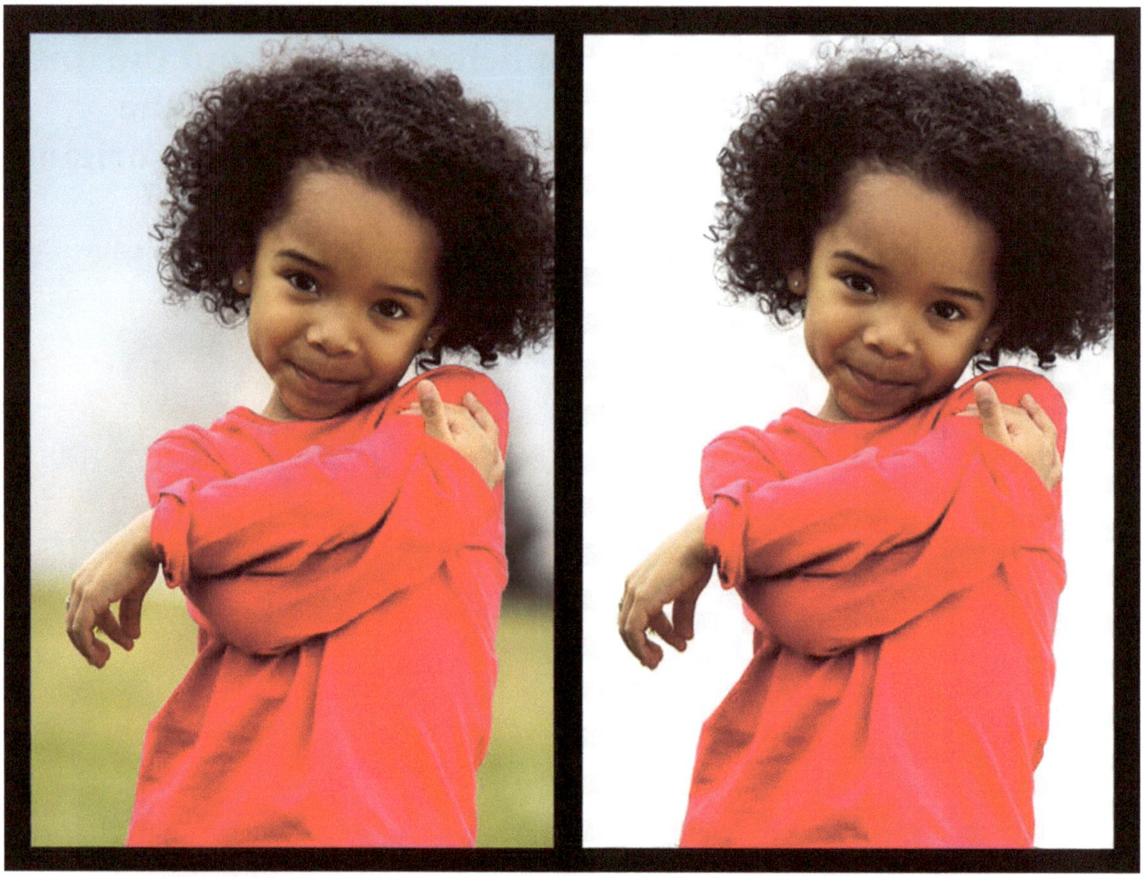

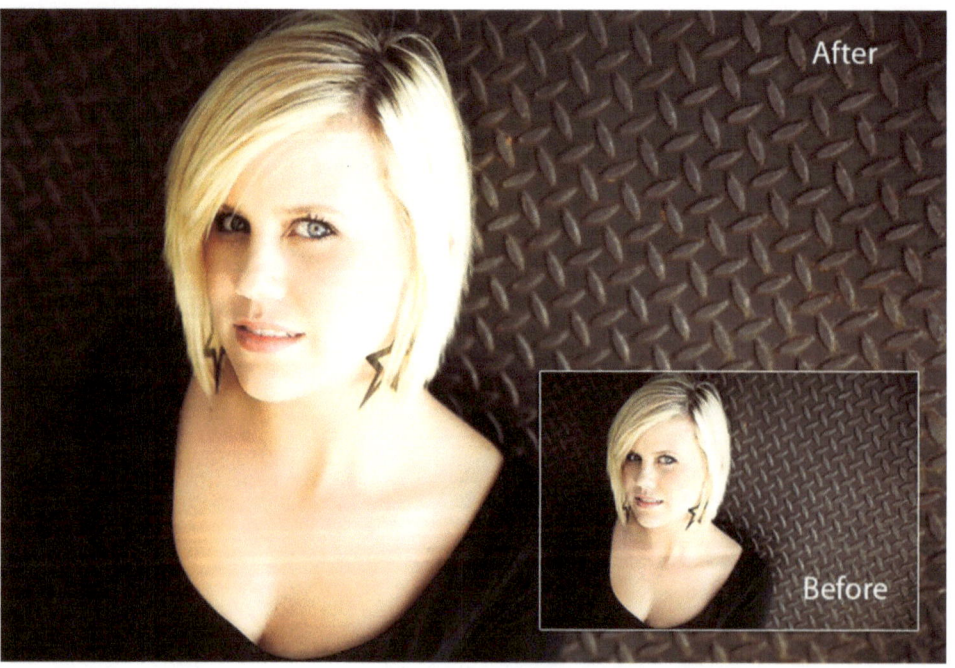

After

Before

onOne Software, Photo Tools 2.5 tinting treatment

onOne Software, Photo Frames 4.5, Plug-In

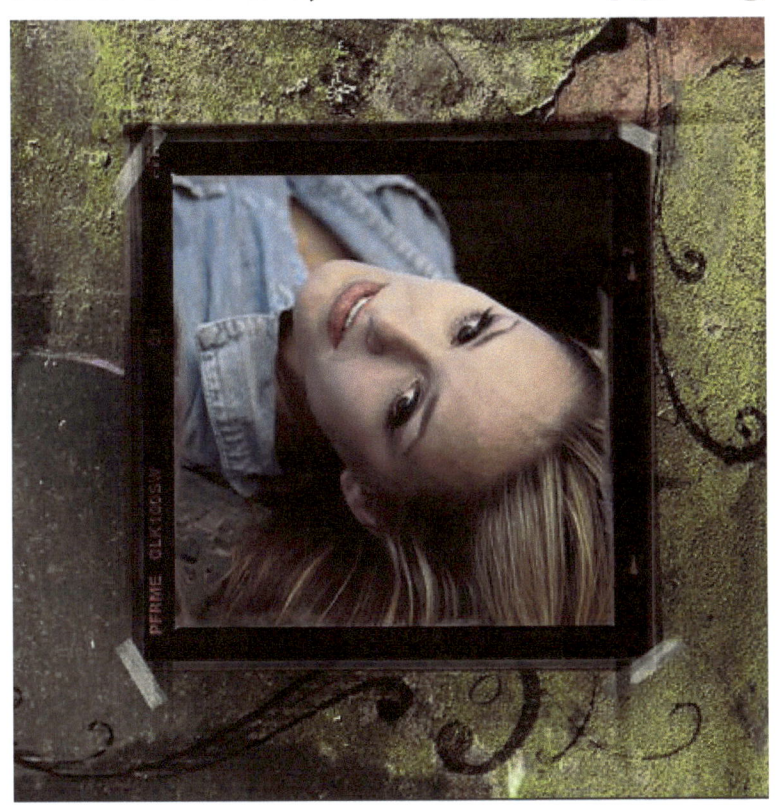

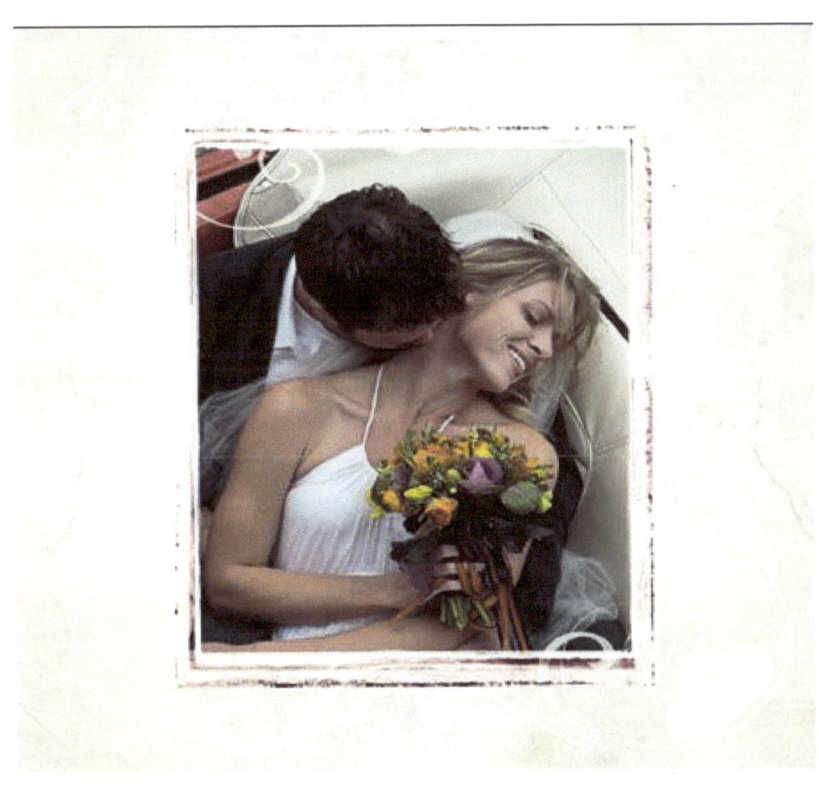

onOne Software, Photo Tune 3, Plug-In, Before & After photos

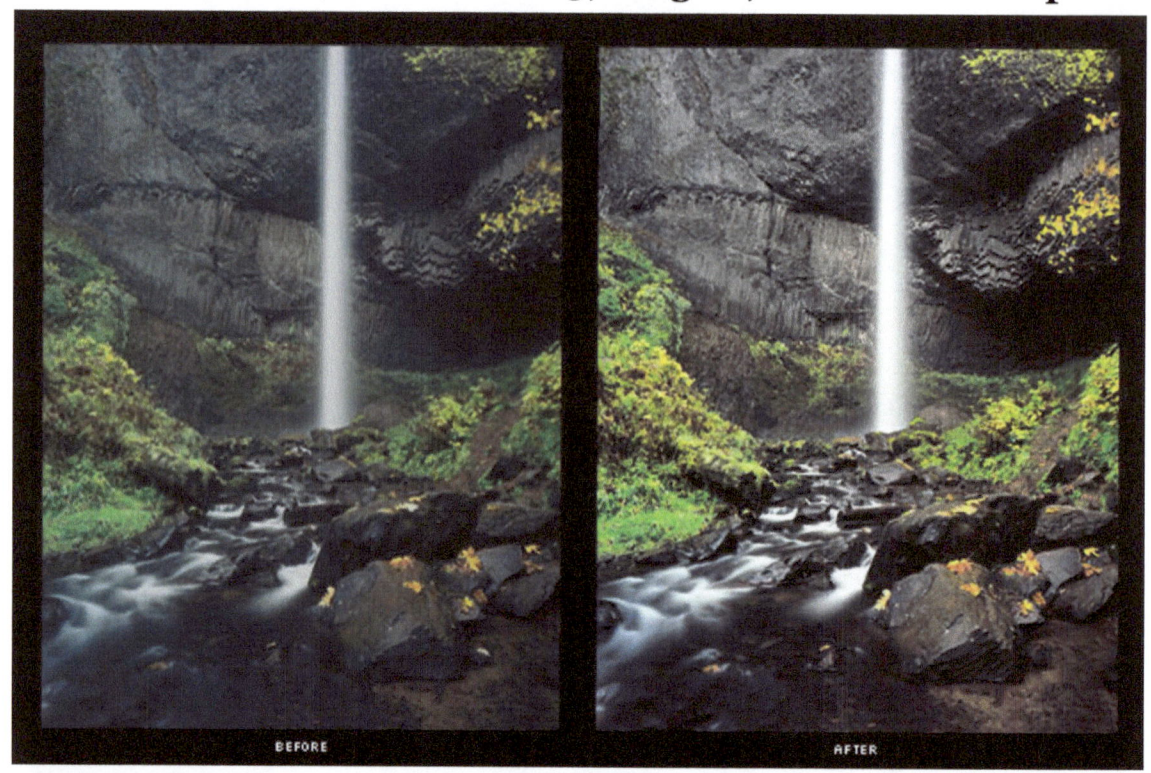

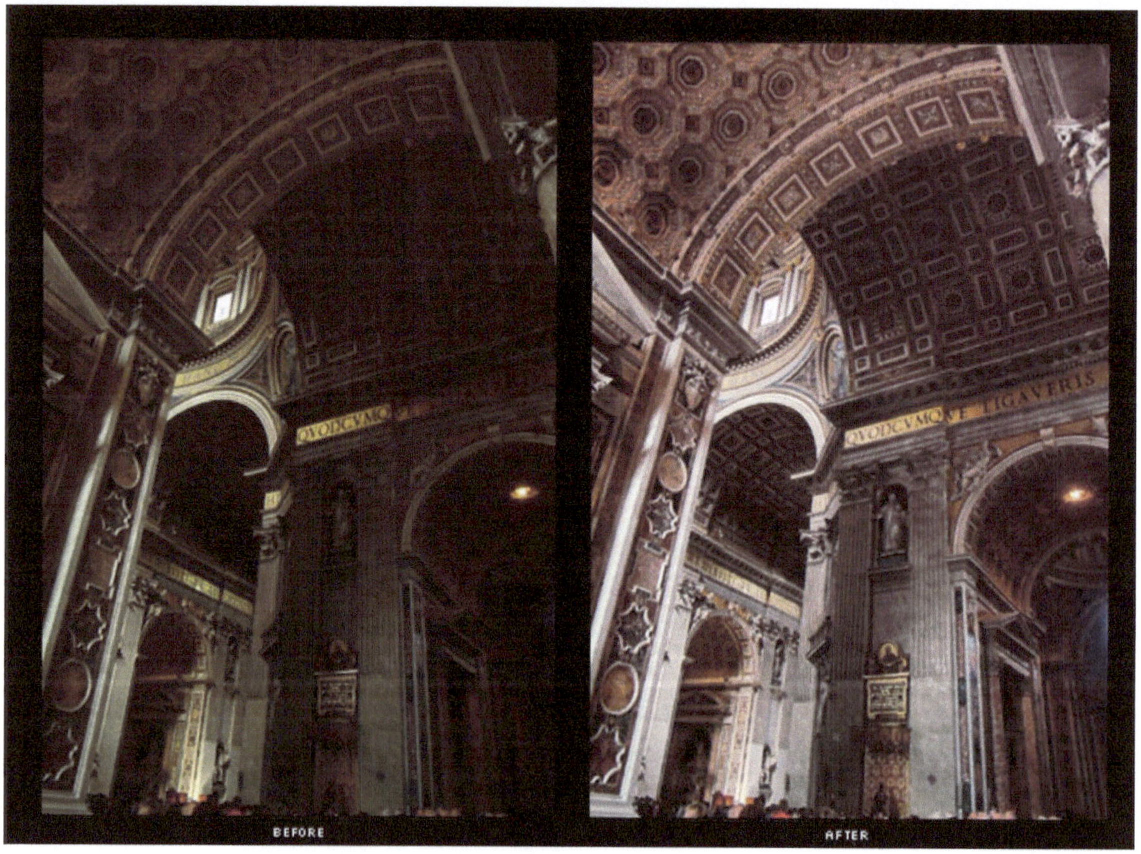

onOne Software, Photo Tools 2.5, Before and After photos

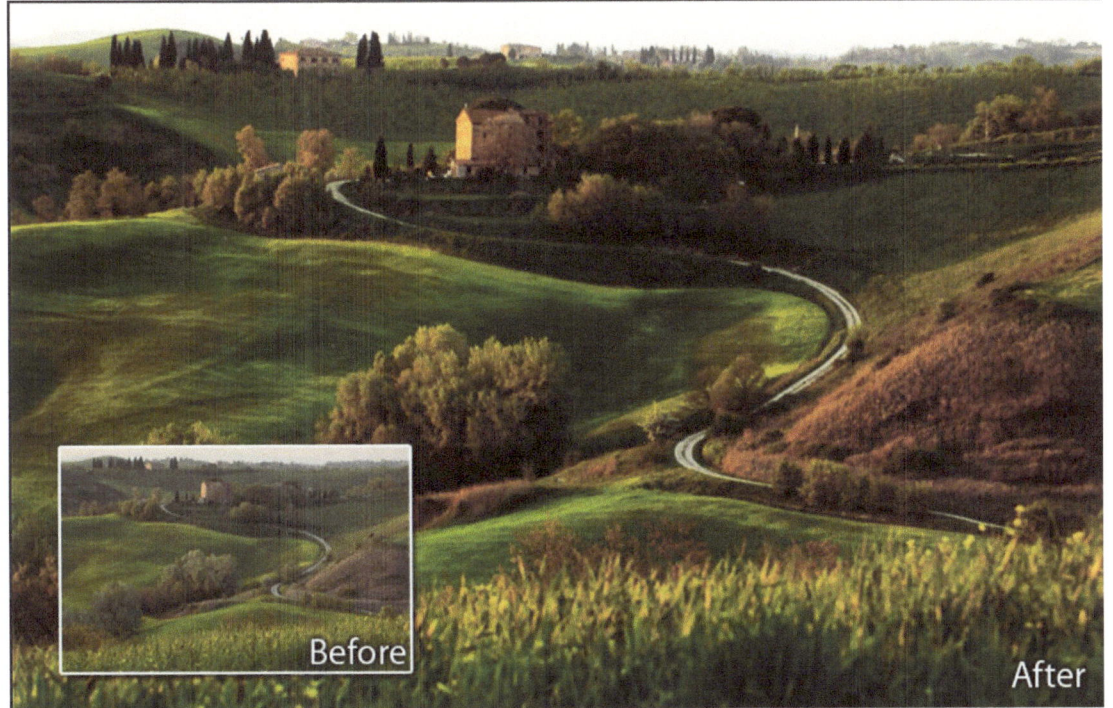

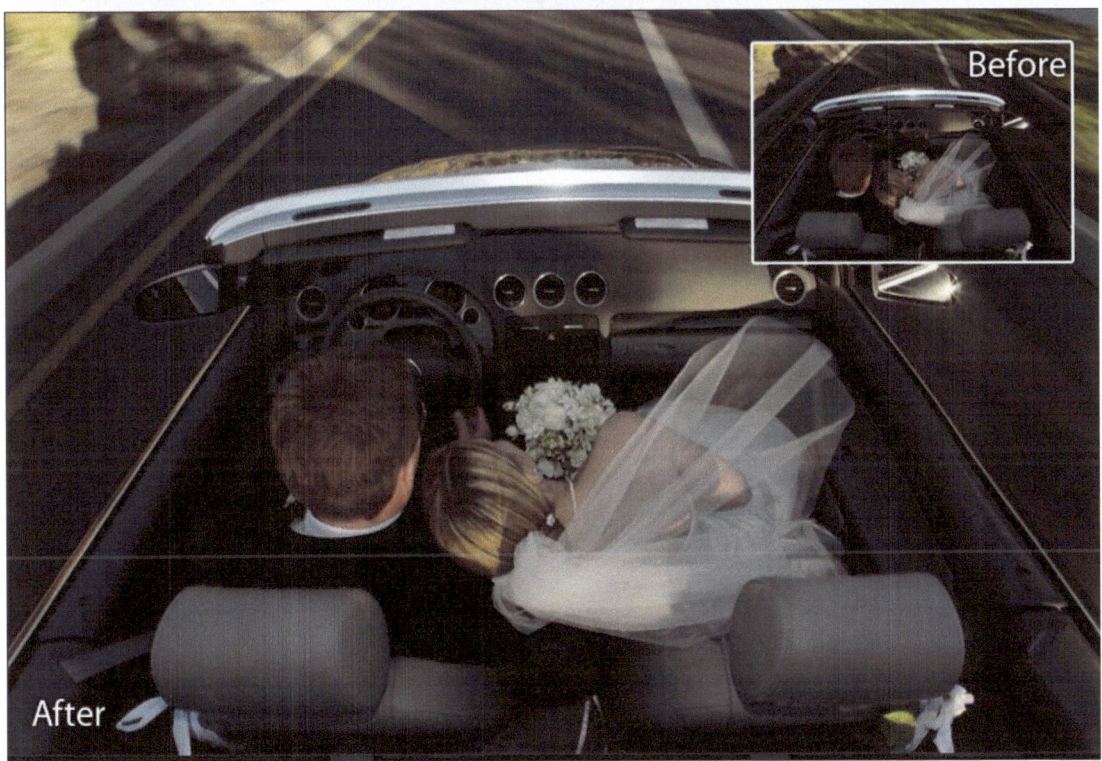

onOne Software, Photo Tools 2.5, Image Optimization

onOne Software, Focal Point 2, gives you control of the focus
. It creates realistic selective focus, depth-of-field and
vignette effects that draws the viewers right to the center of
attention. Both photos below show this effect of vignette
and depth of field.

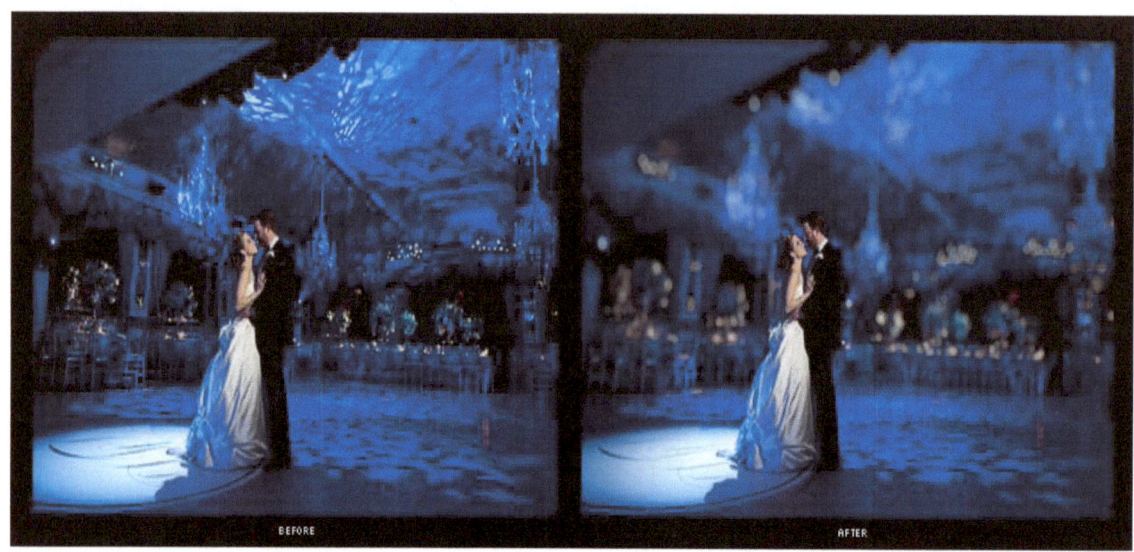

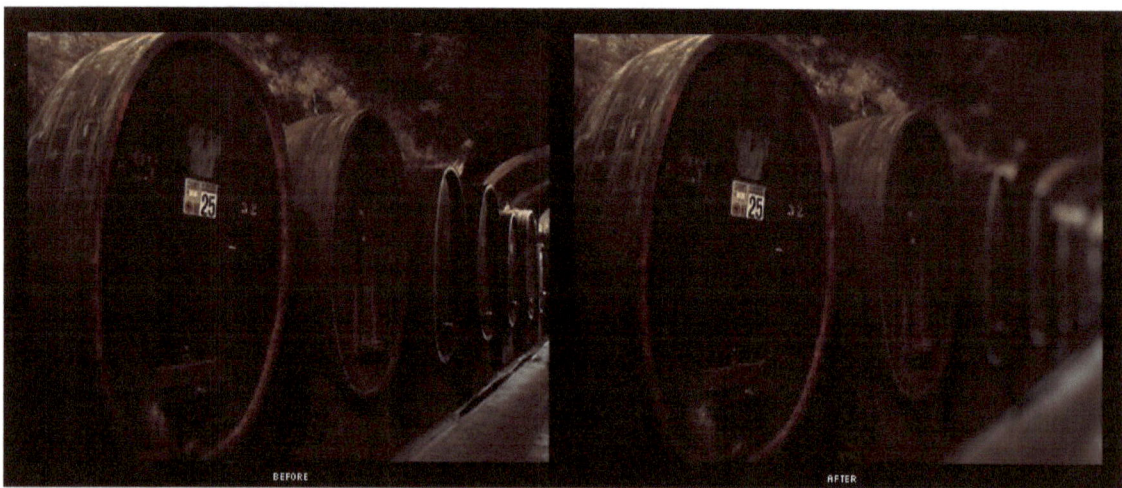

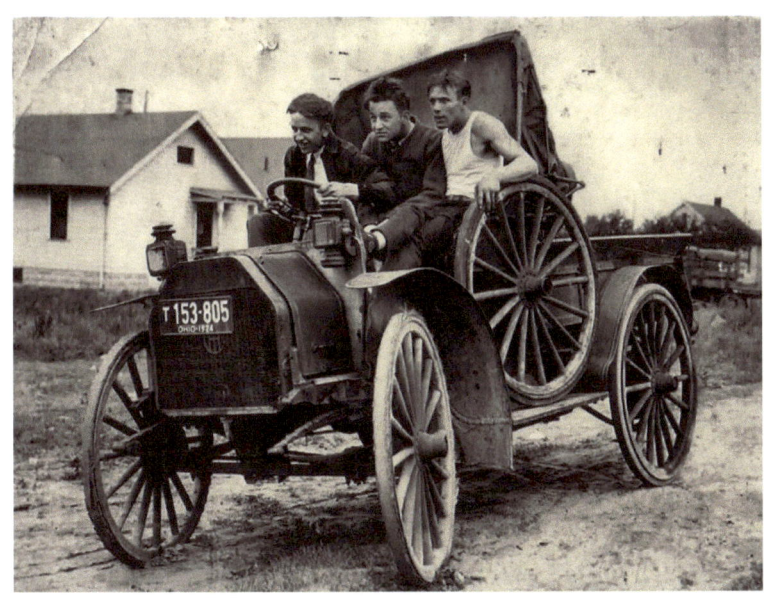

Antique Photo

Photoshop CS5 Spot Healing Brush, Nik Software Silver Efex Pro, Plug-In

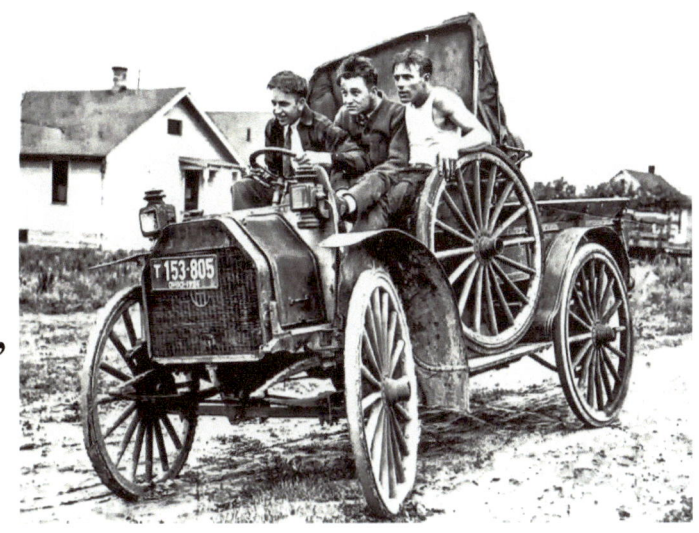

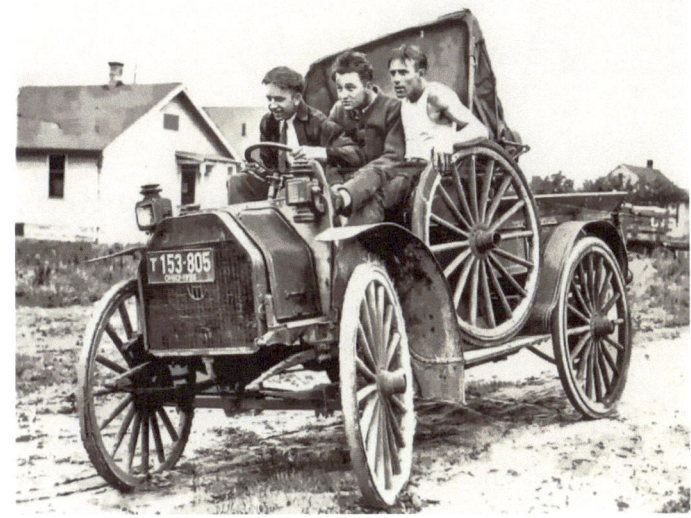

Photoshop CS5, Nik Software Simplify 3, Watercolor, Plug-In

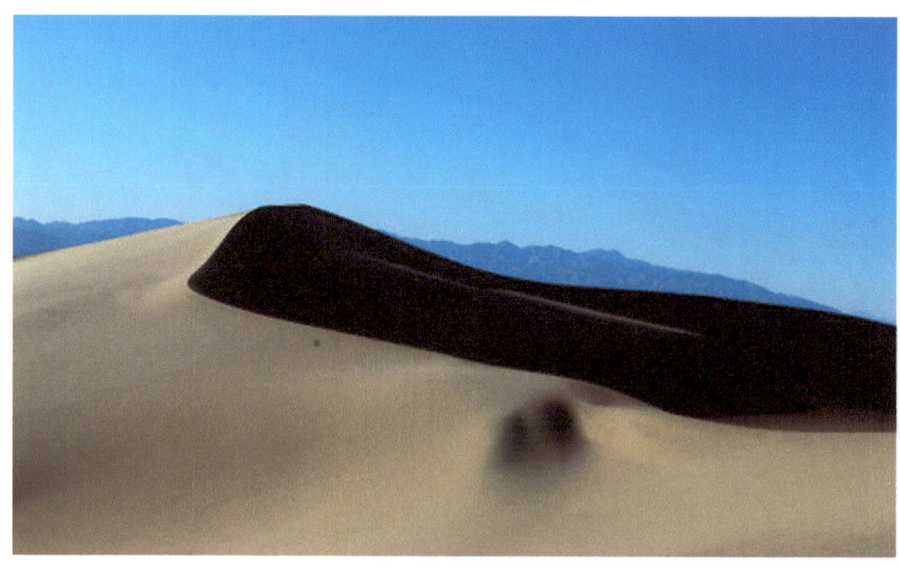

Original Photo

**Photoshop CS5
Topaz Labs
Detail 2,
DeNoise 5, Plug-In**

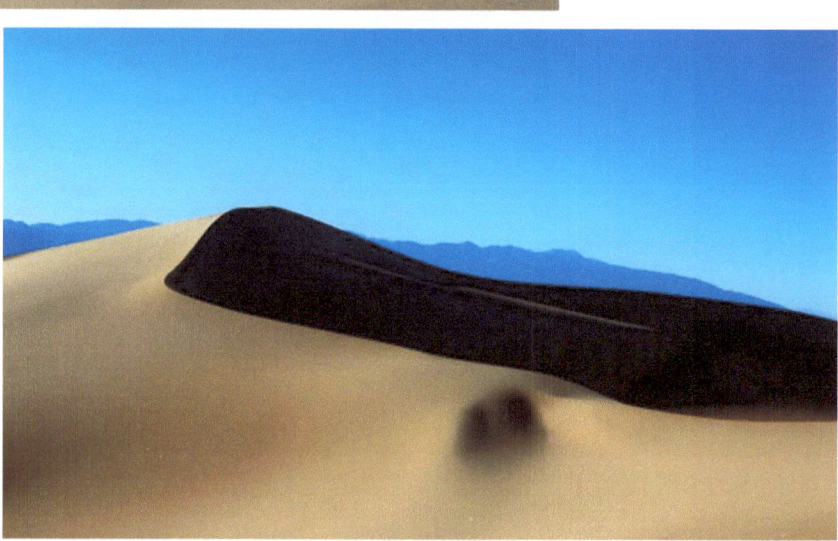

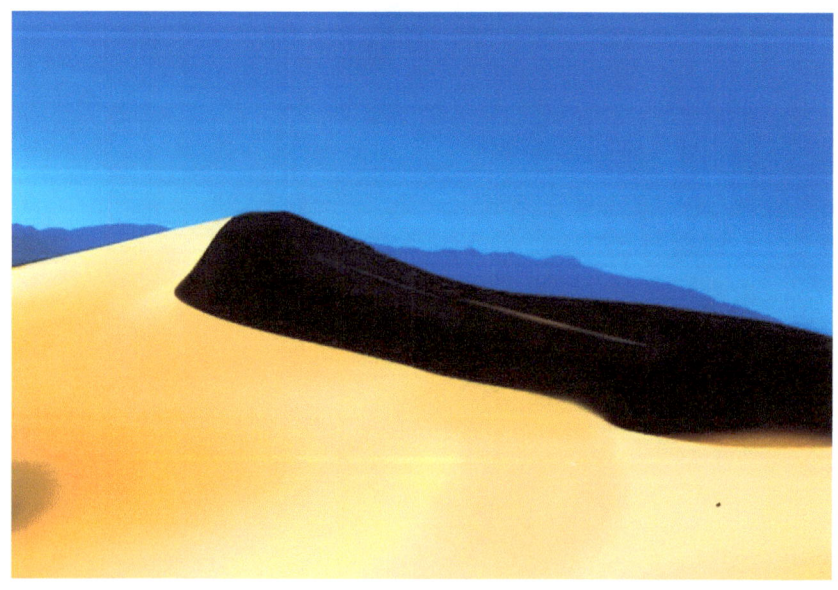

**Photoshop CS5
Spot Healing Brush
Topaz Adjust 4
Smooth & Flat,
Plug-In**

Original Photo

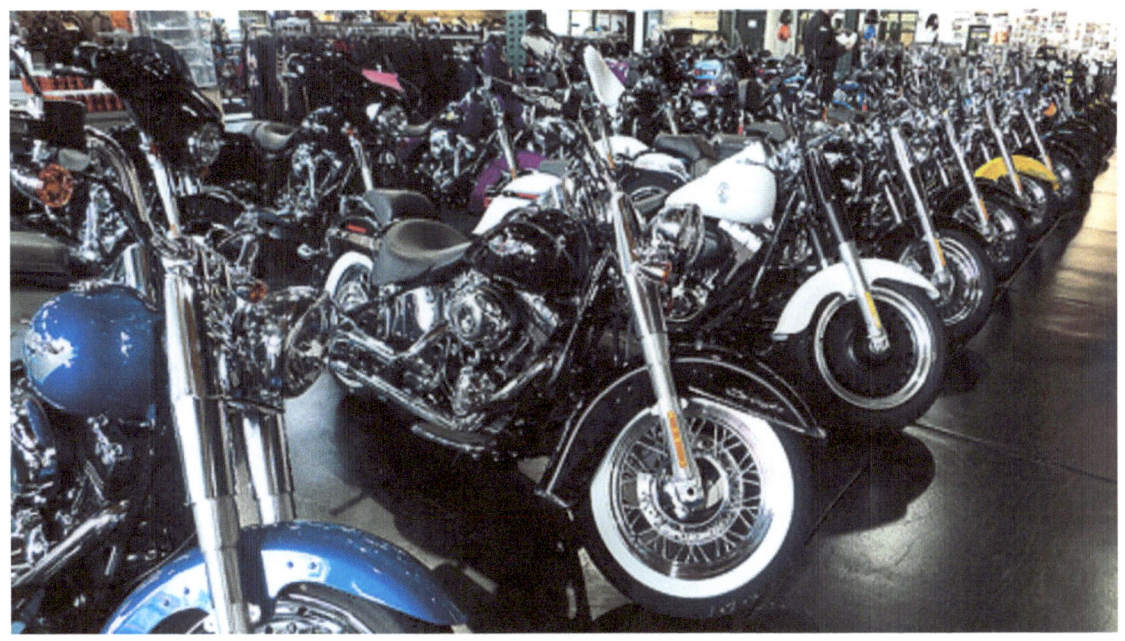

Photoshop CS5
Topaz Labs, Adjust 4, Plug-In

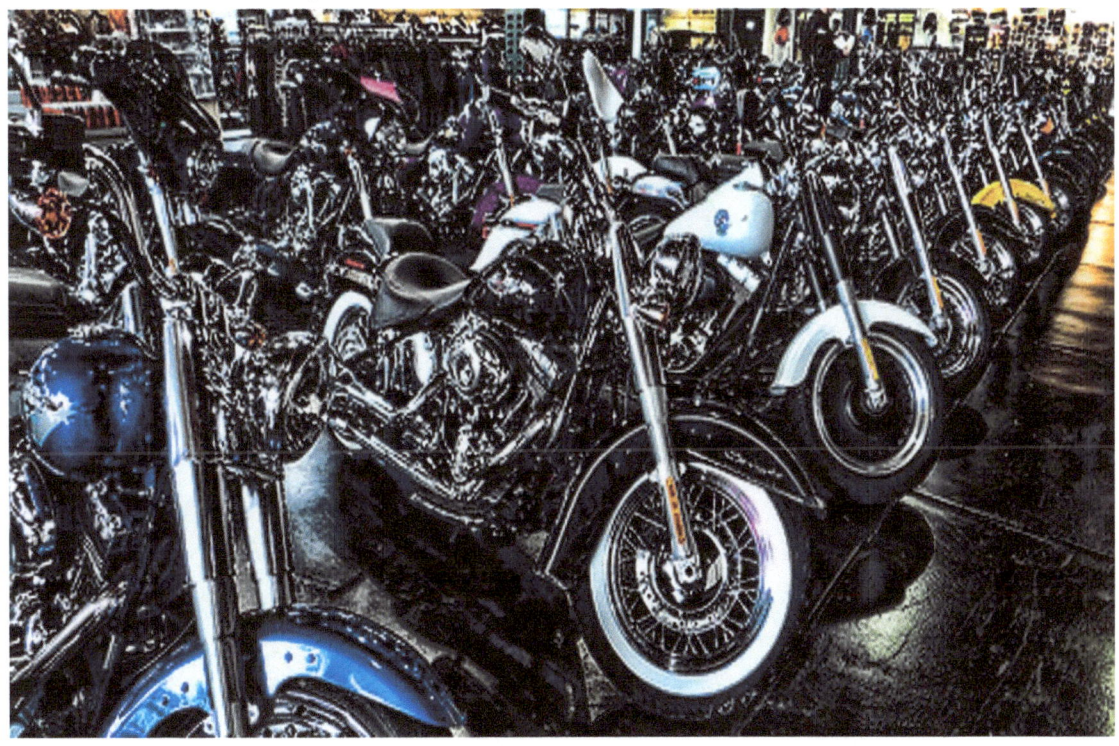

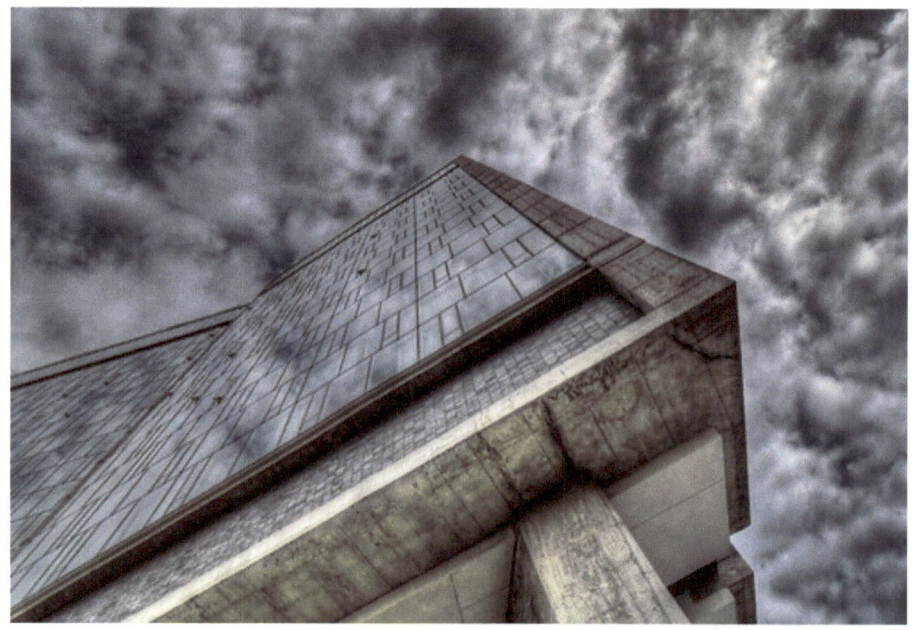

Original Photo

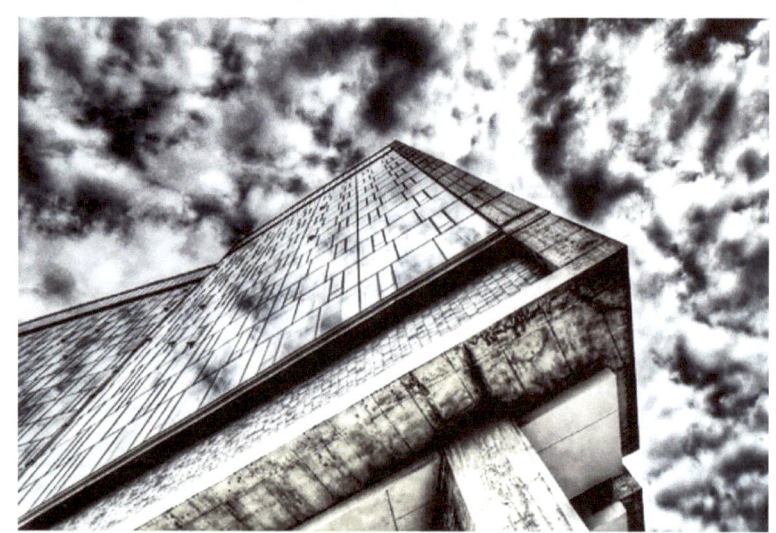

Photoshop CS5, Nik Software, Photo Efex Pro 3, Bleach Bypass Plug-In

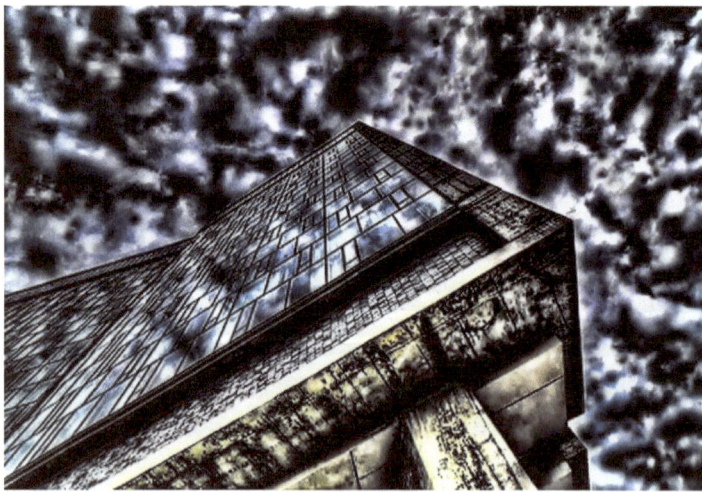

Photoshop CS5, Topaz Labs, Adjust 4, Exposure Correction, Nik Software, Define 2, Plug-In

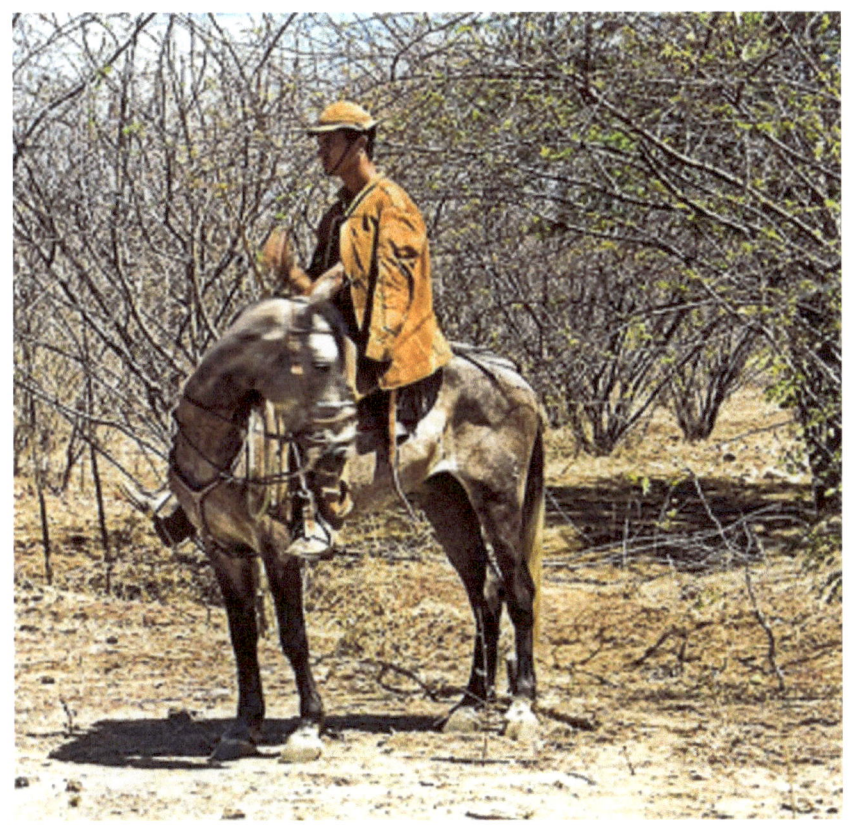

Original Photo

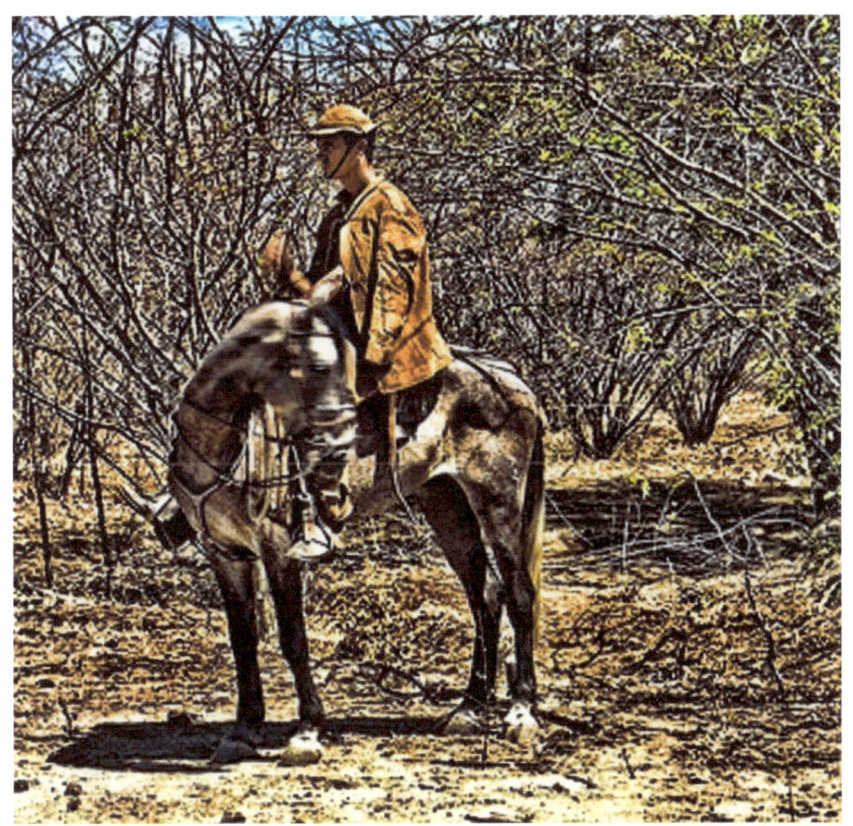

**Photoshop CS5
Topaz Labs, Adjust
4, Spicify, Nik
Software Viveza 2
Plug-In**

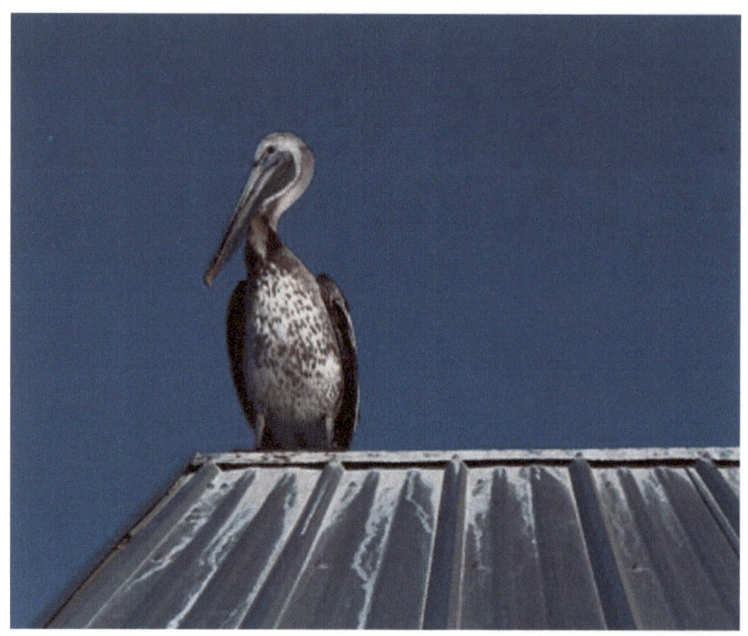

Original Photo, Photoshop CS5, Cropped and Noise reduction

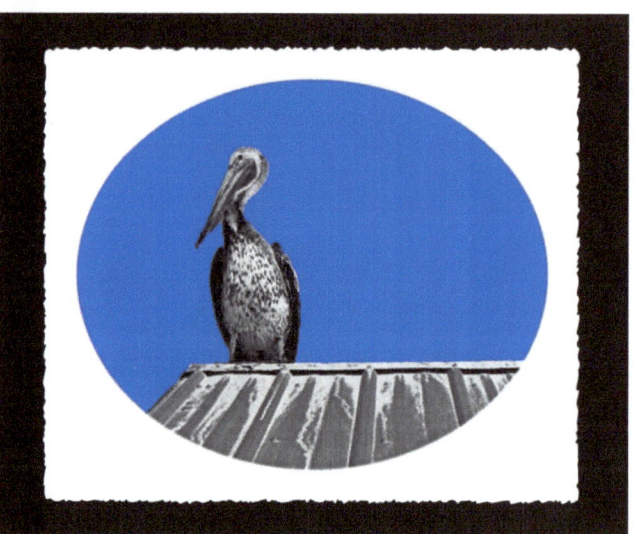

Photoshop CS5, Panos FX Action, Plug-In

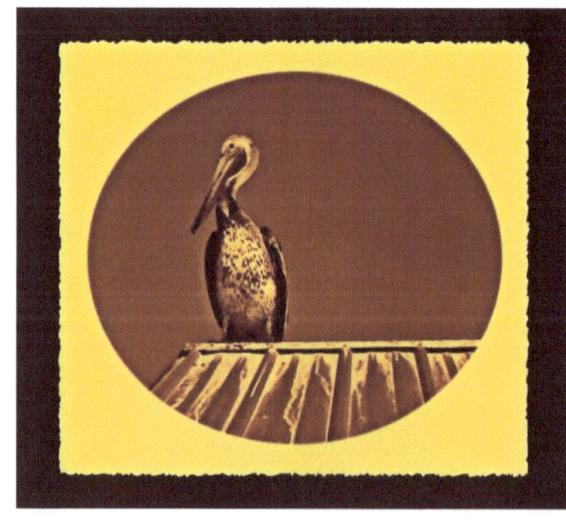

Photoshop CS5, Panos FX Action onOne Software ,Photo Tools 2.5 Nik Software, Color Efex Pro 3, Plug-In

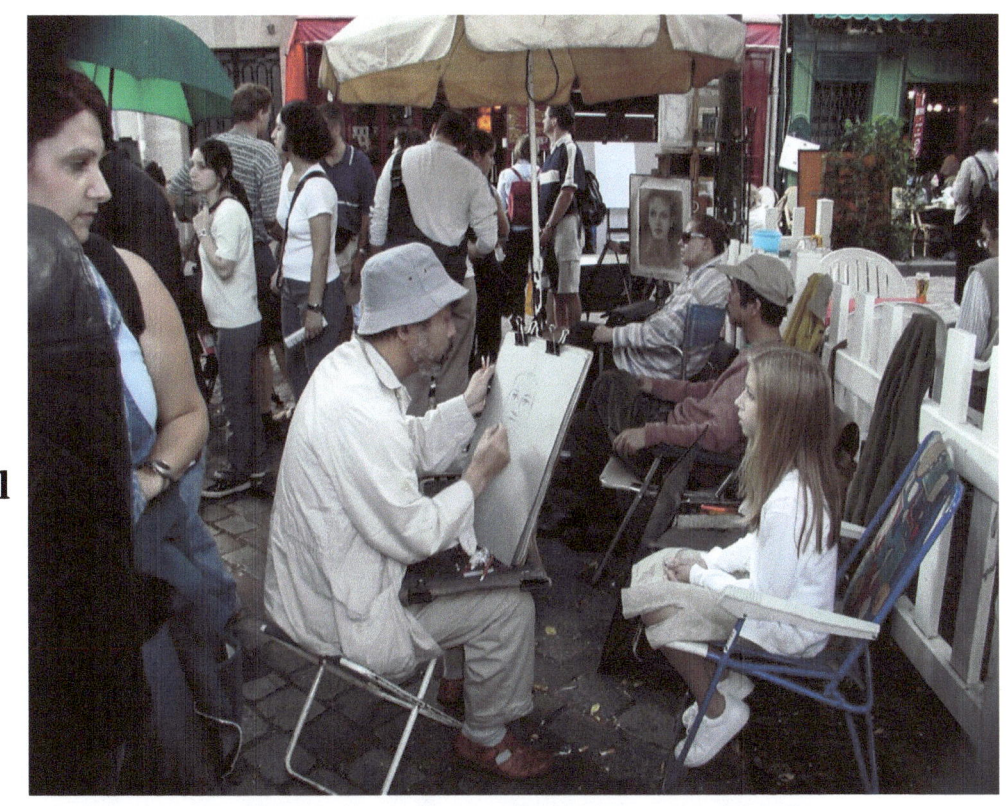

Original Photo

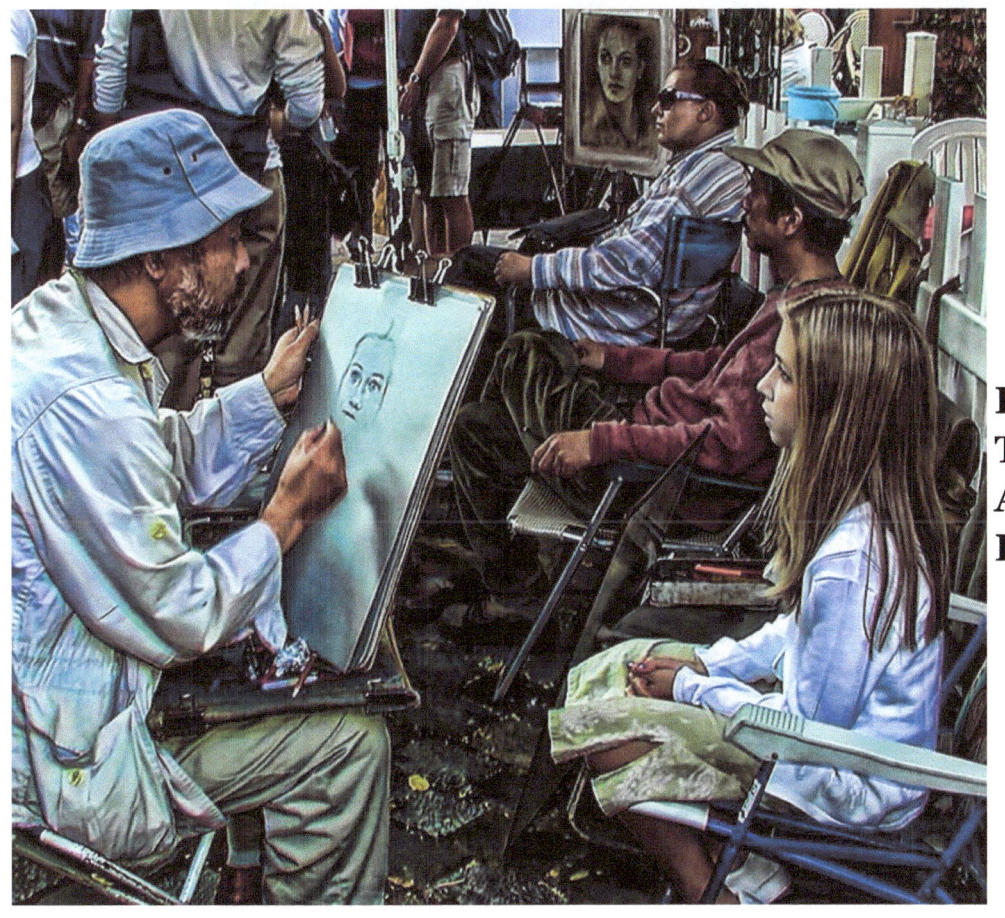

Photoshop CS5 Topaz Labs, Adjust 4, Plug-In

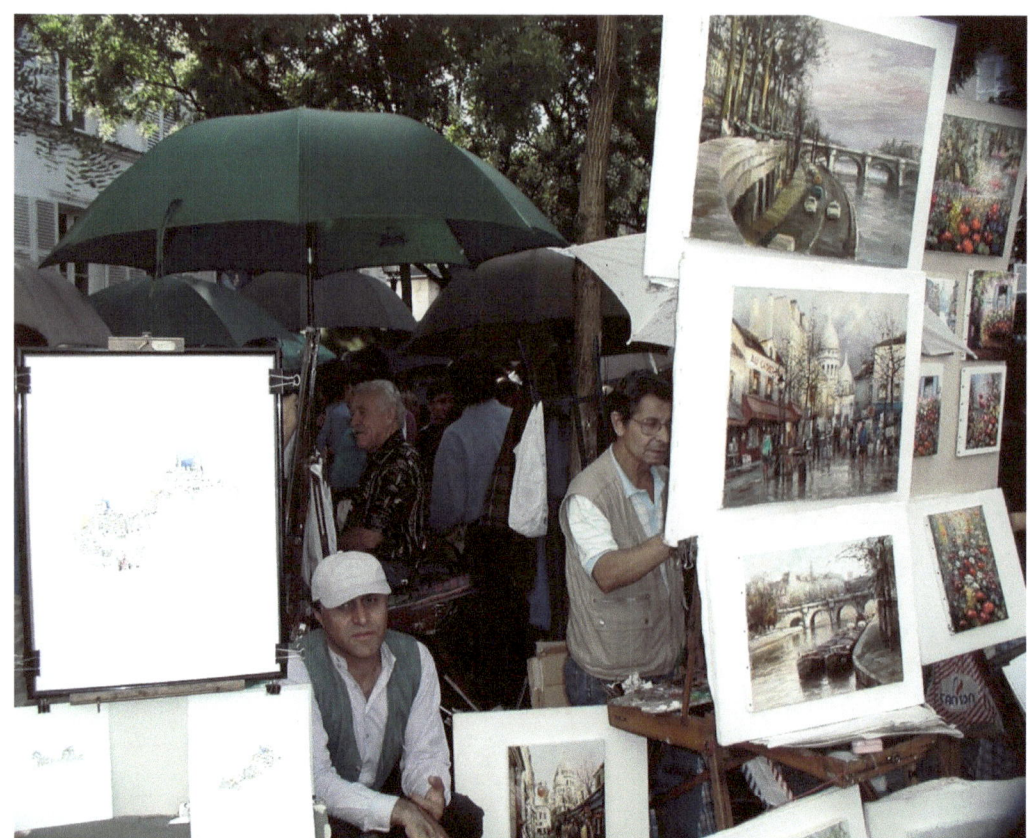

Original Photo

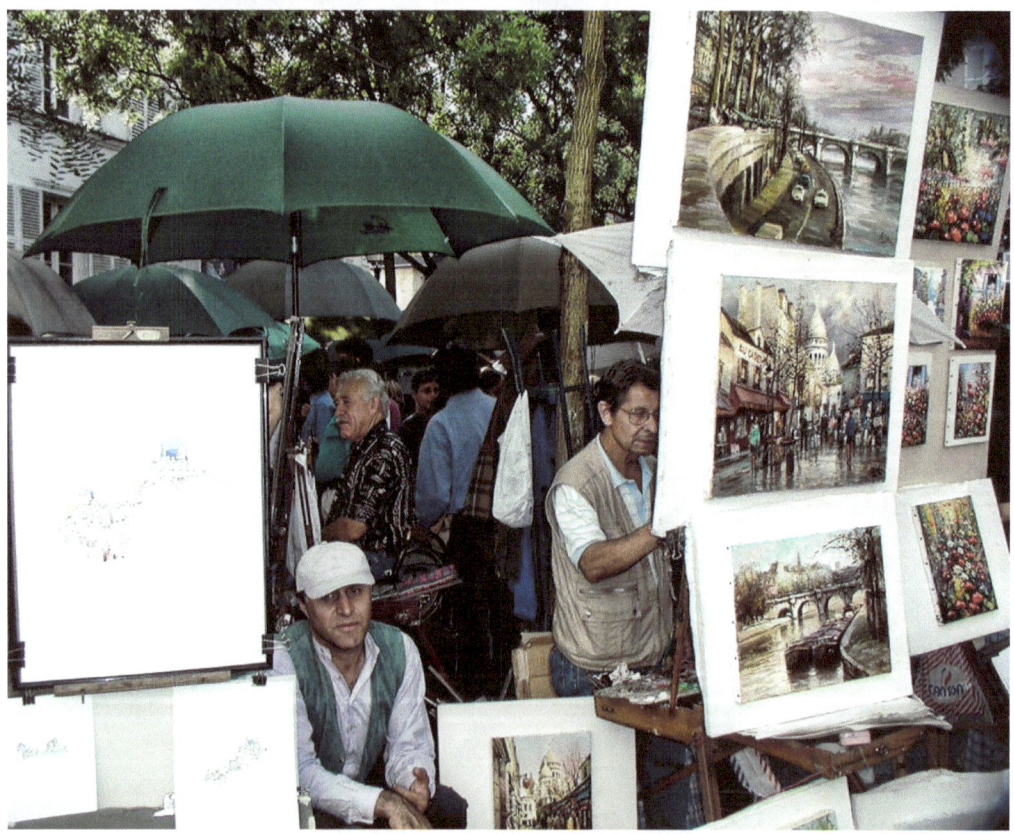

Photoshop CS5, Topaz Labs, Adjust, Vibrance, Plug-In

Original Photo

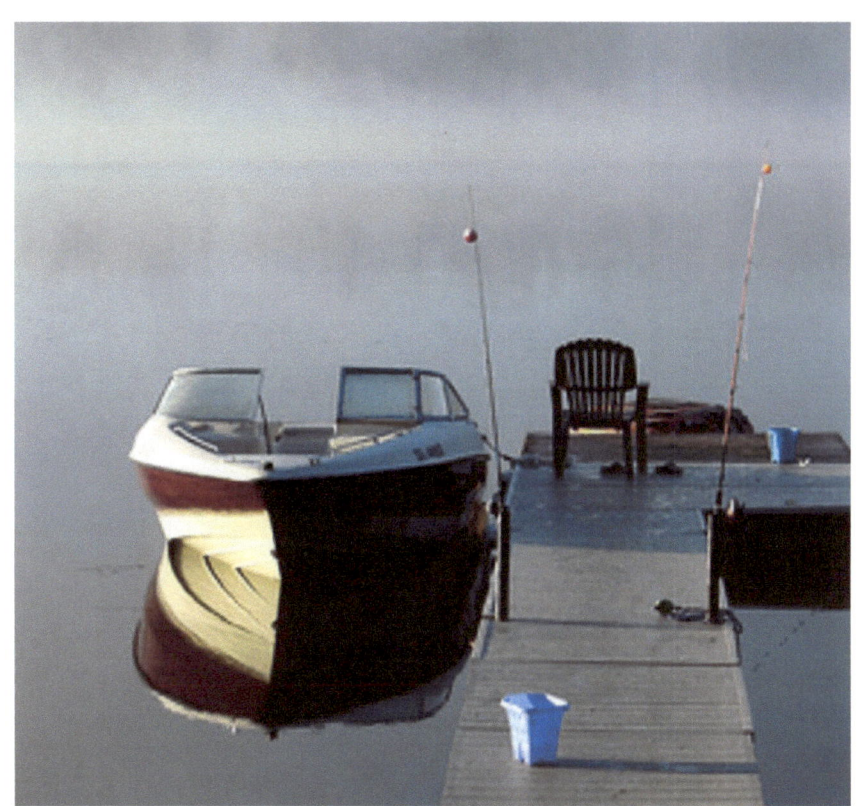

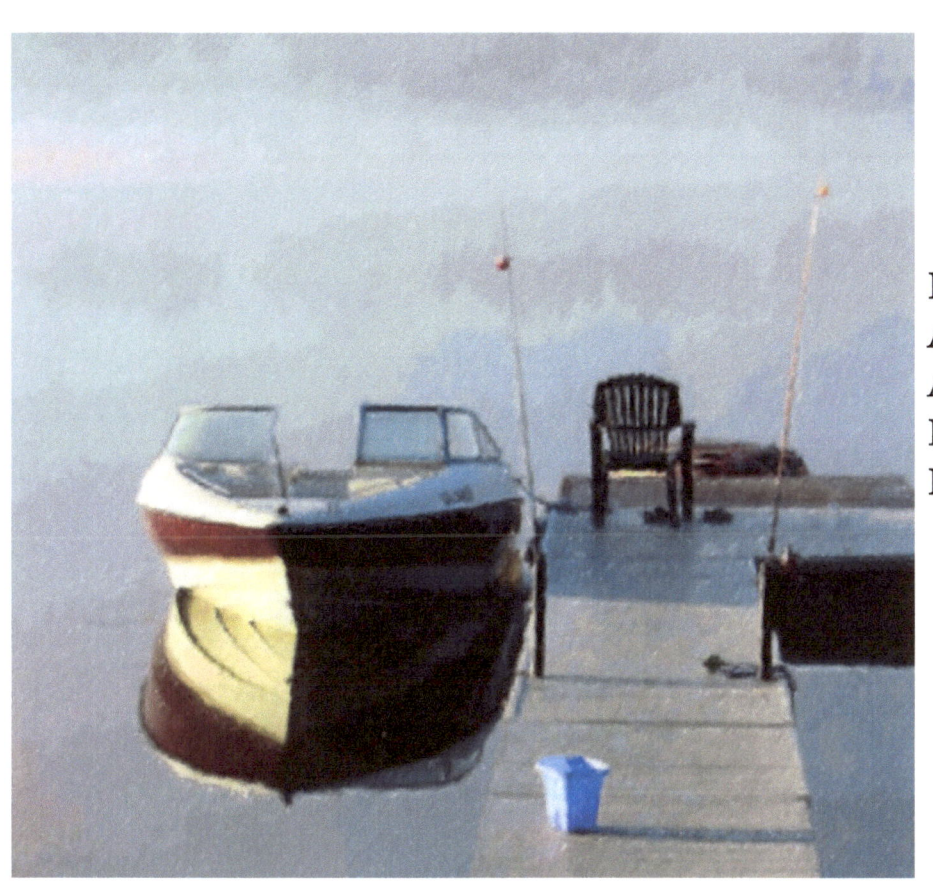

Photoshop CS5, Ailen Skin Snap Art, Colored Pencil Sketch, Plug– In

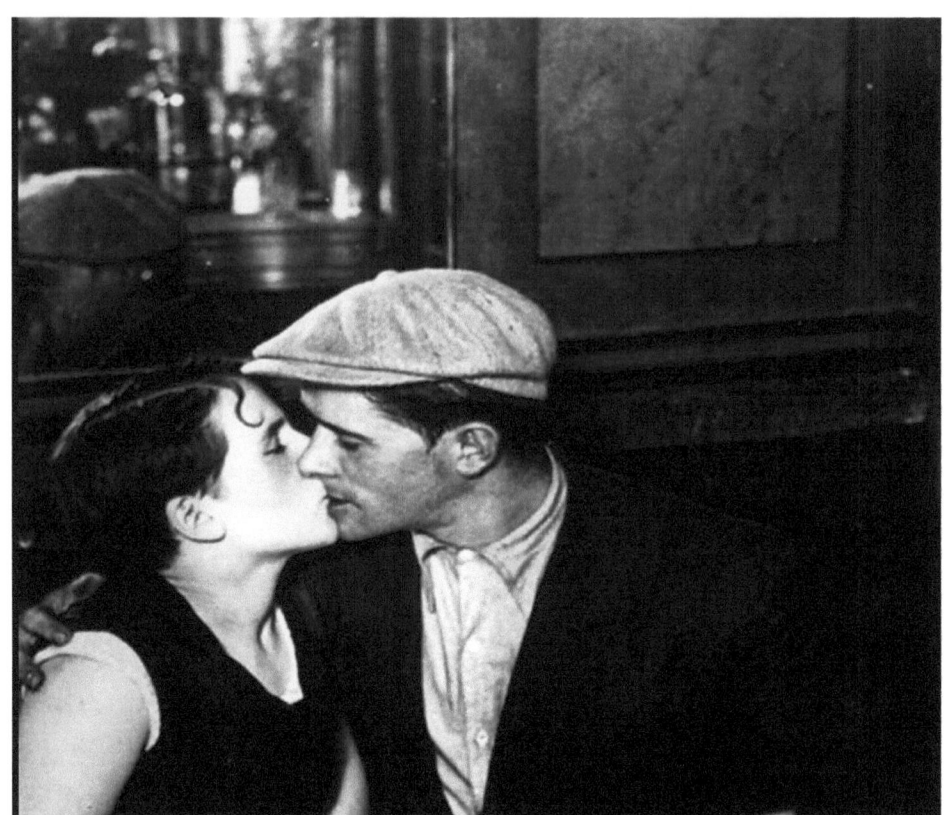

Original Photo

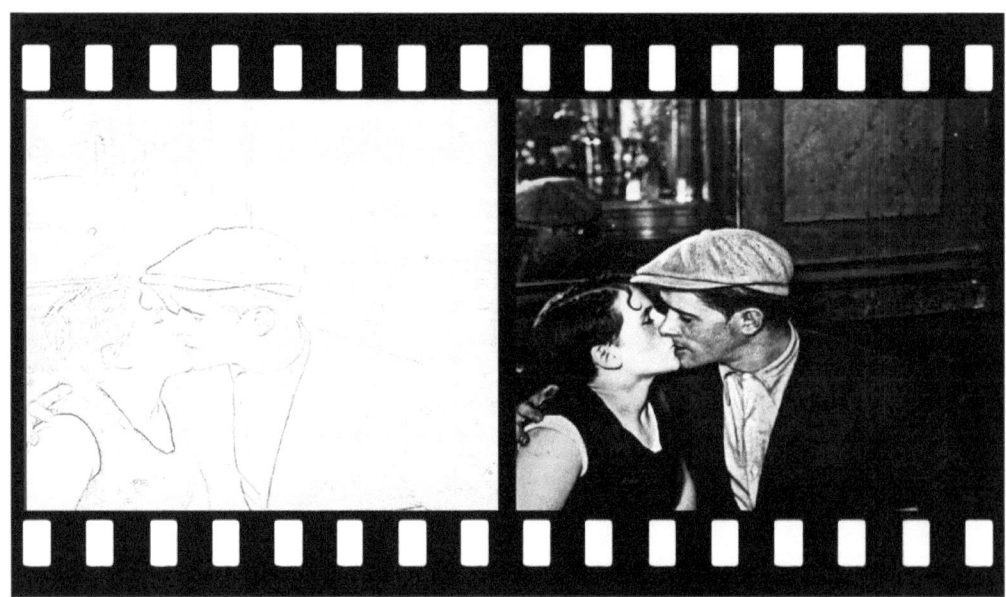

Panos FX Sketch, Plug-In

Photoshop CS5, onOne Software, Photo Tools 2.5, Panos FX Film Strip, Plug-In

Original Photo

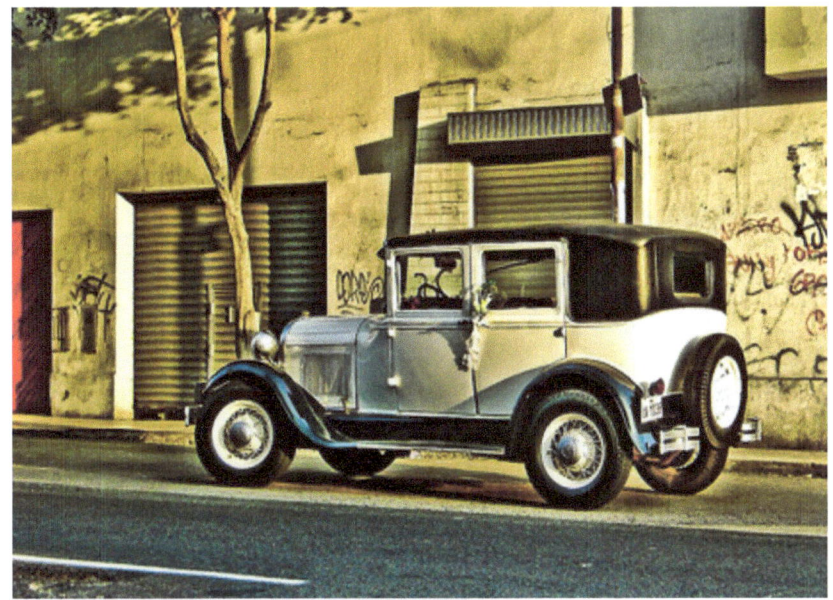

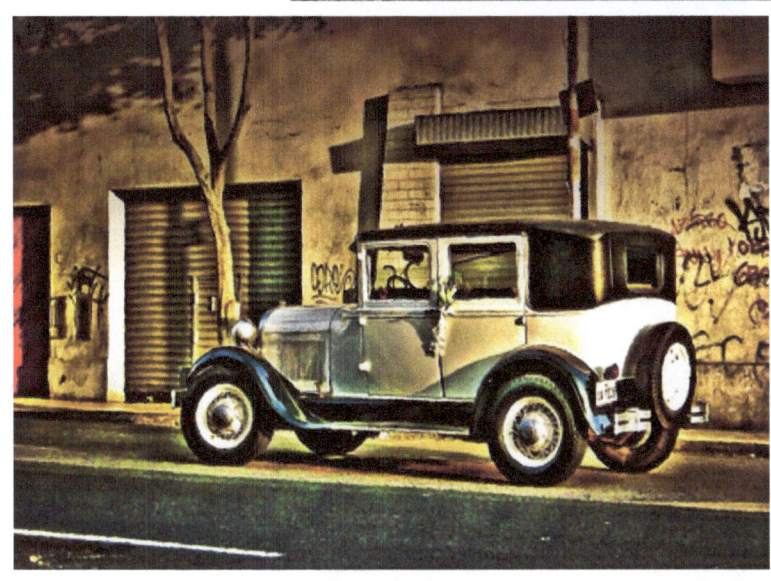

Photoshop CS5, onOne Software, Photo Tools 2.5, Presets, Plug-In

Photoshop CS5, Topaz Labs, Smooth & Flat, Plug-In

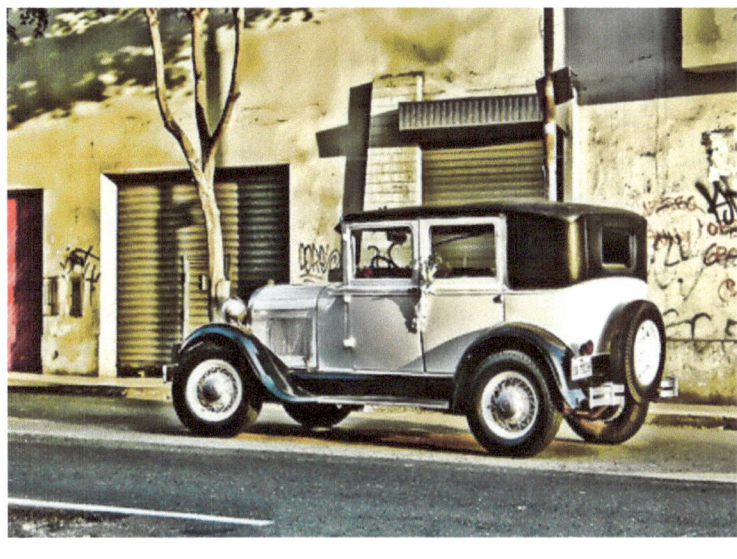

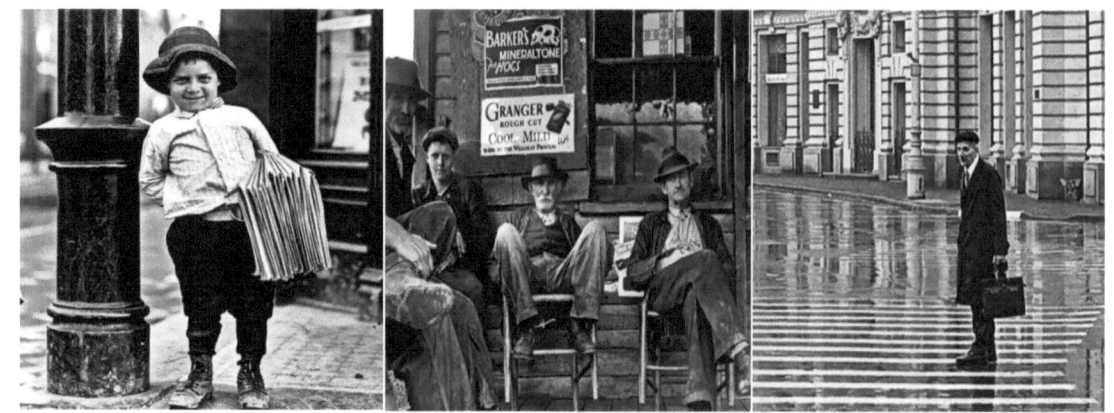

Original Photos

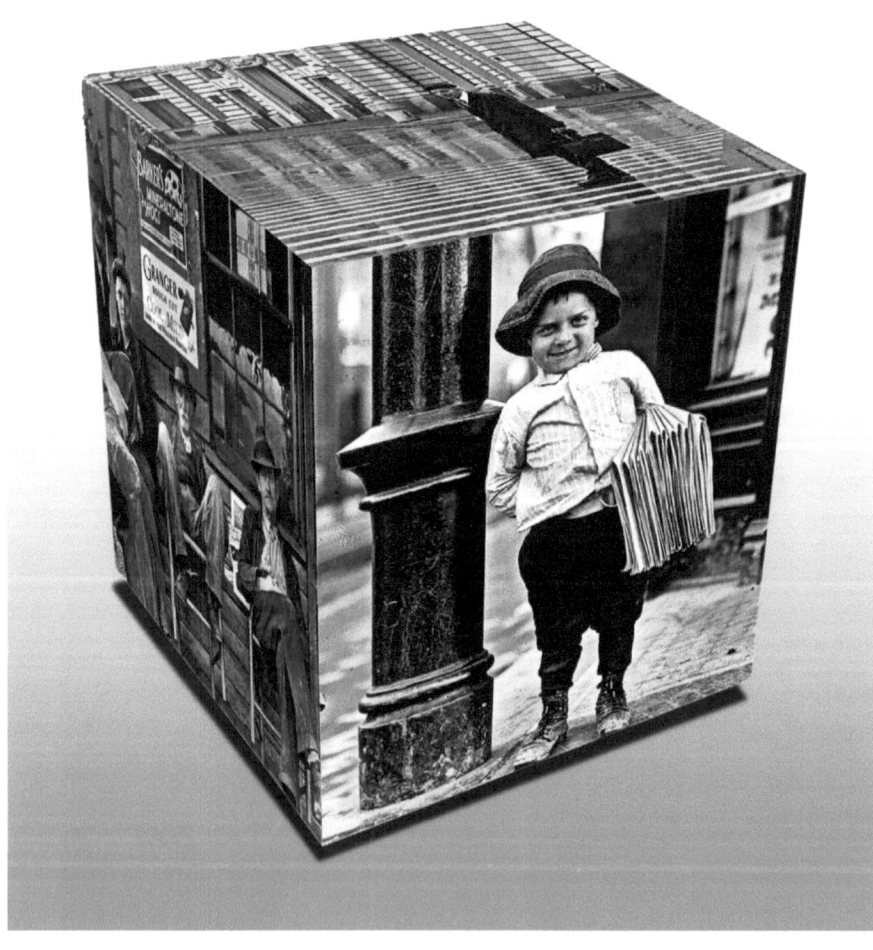

Photoshop CS5, Panos FX Cube 3, all three photos enhanced with onOne Software, Photo Tools 2.5, Plug-In

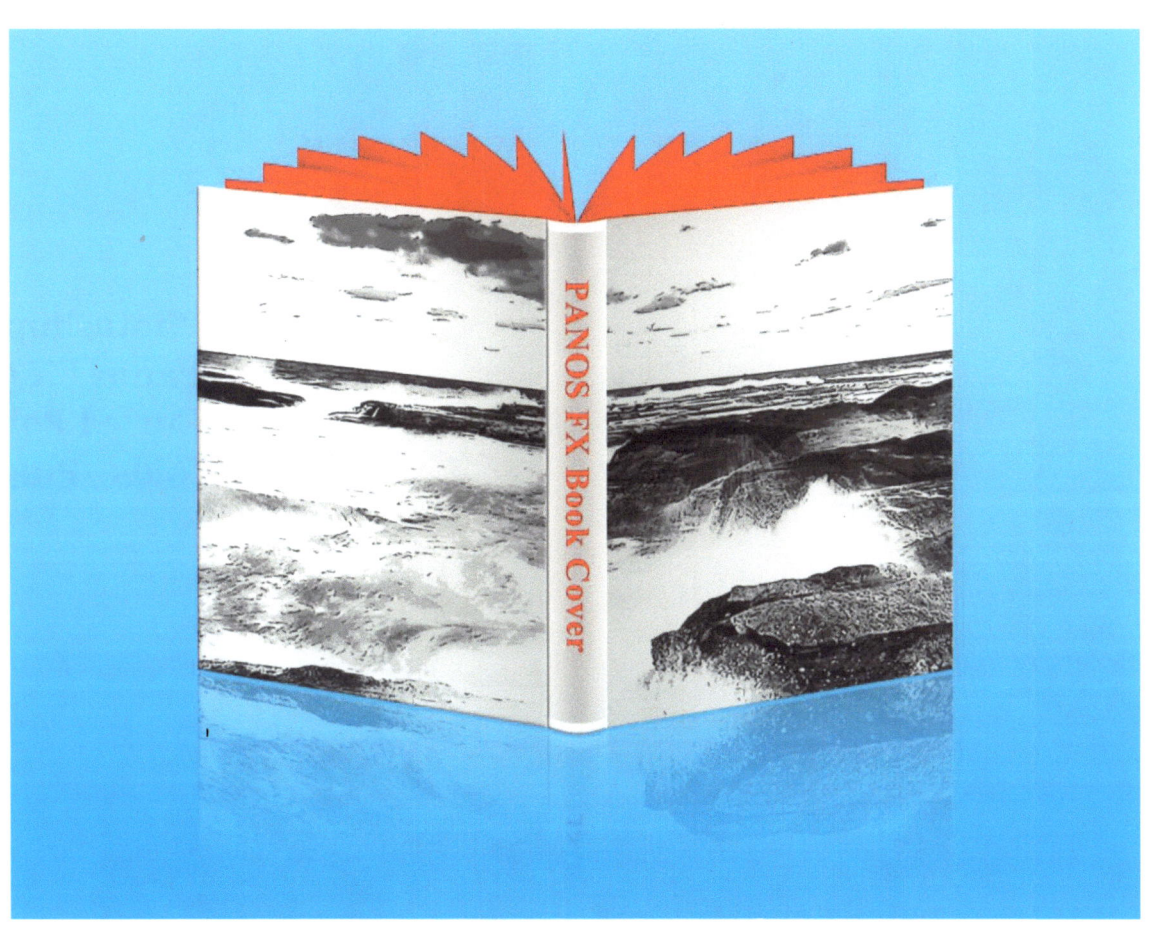

PANOS FX Book Cover

Photoshop CS5
Nik Software
Silver Efex Pro
Panos FX Action
Book Cover
One Image

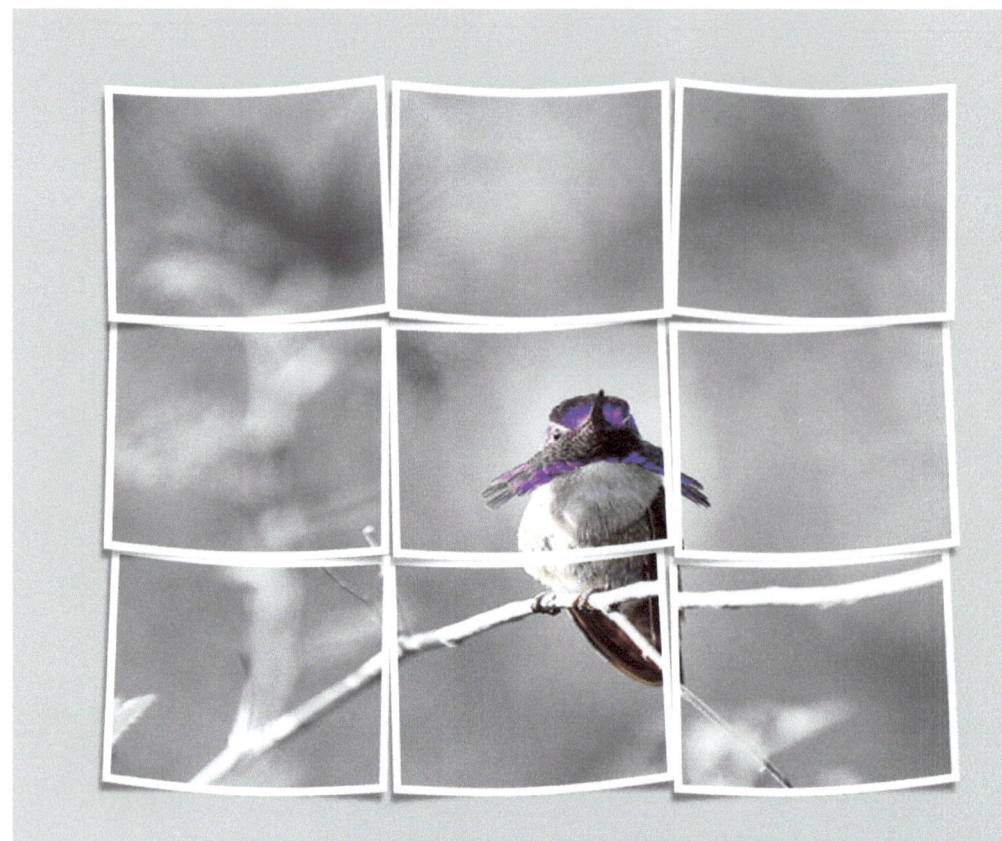

**Photoshop CS5
Panos FX 9
Curled Pola-
foids , Plug-In**

**Photoshop CS5
Panos FX 9 Flat
Reflection, Plug-
In**

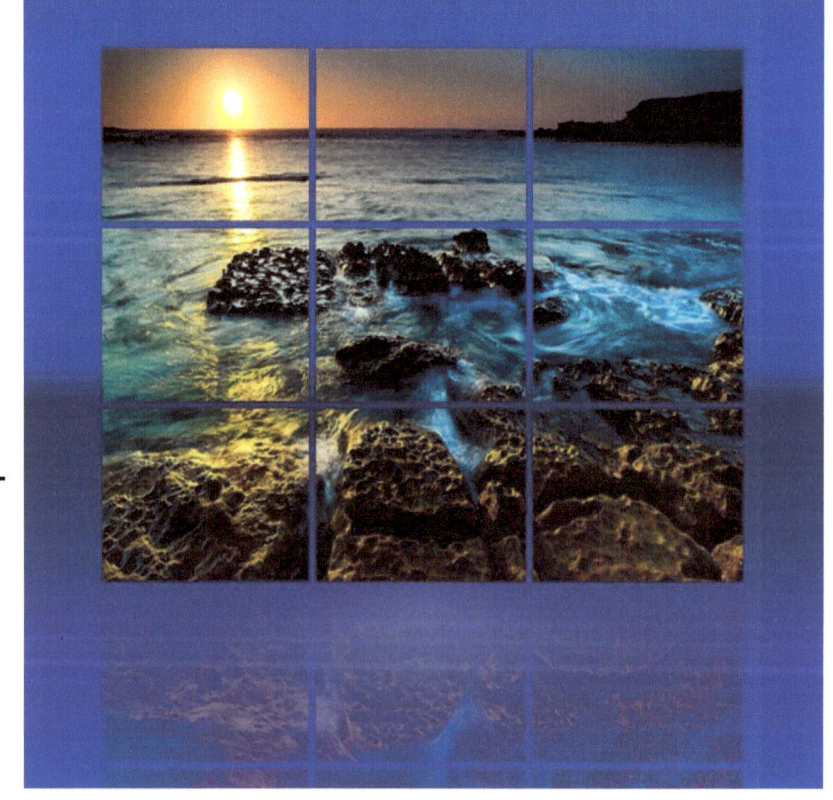

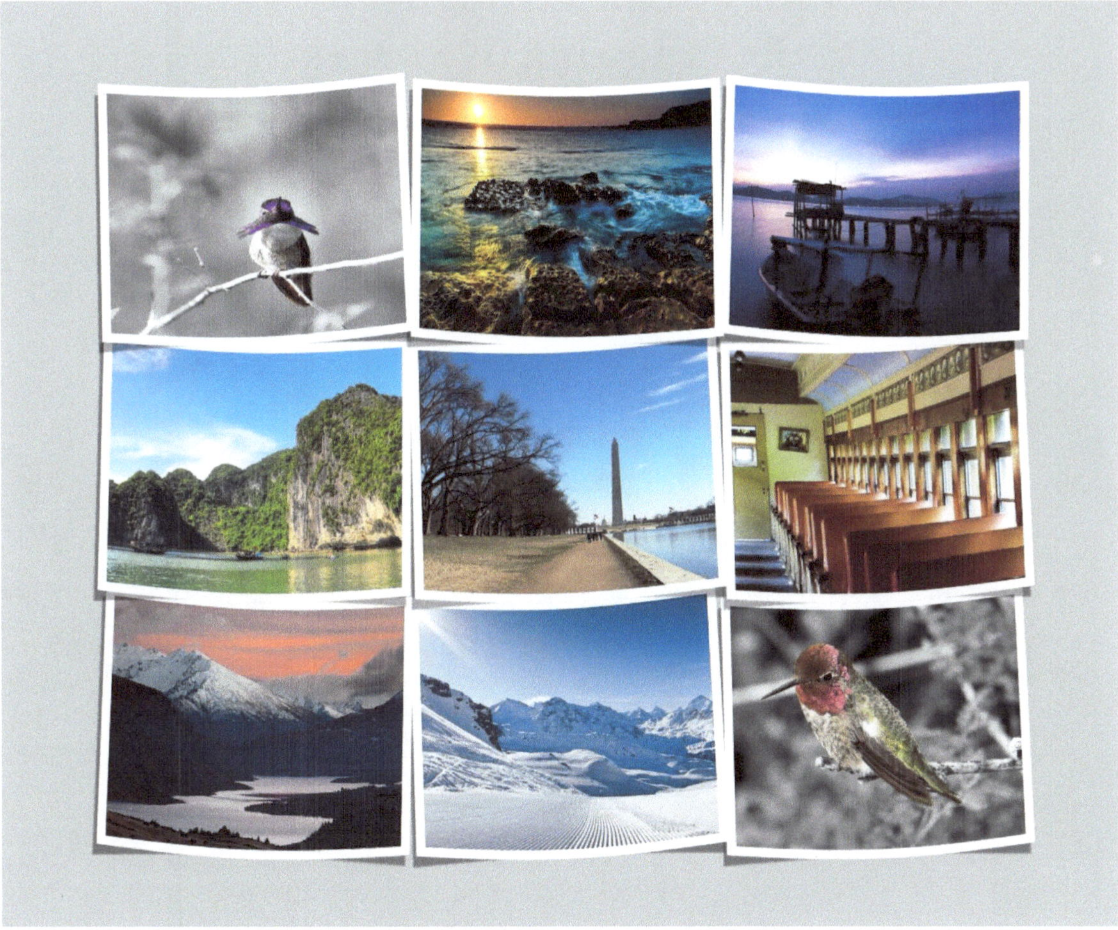

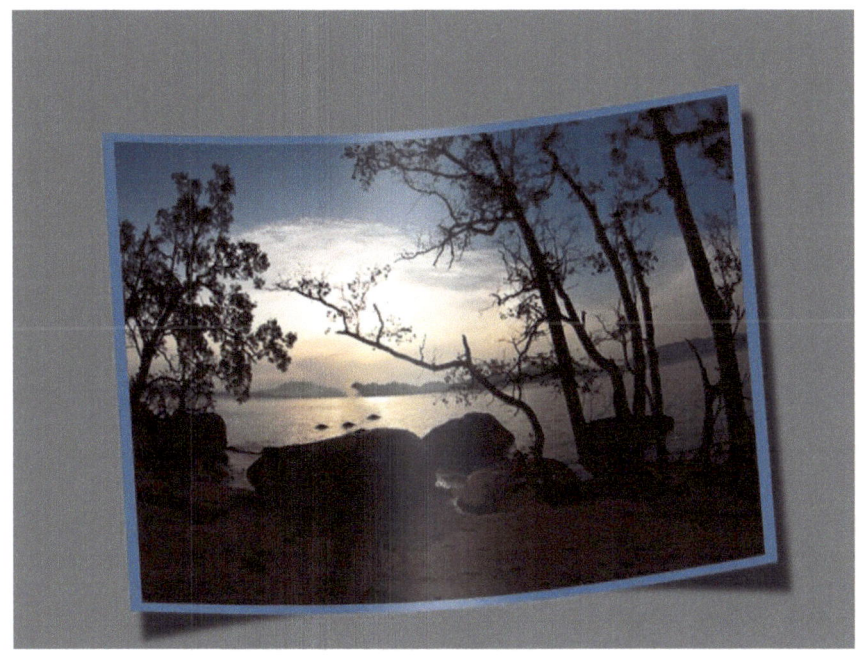

Photoshop CS5, Panos FX 9 curled Polaroid's, Plug-In

**Photoshop CS5
Panos FX
Concave
bottom
shadow, Plug-In**

Work of Rick Sellick using Topaz Labs
On the following five pages

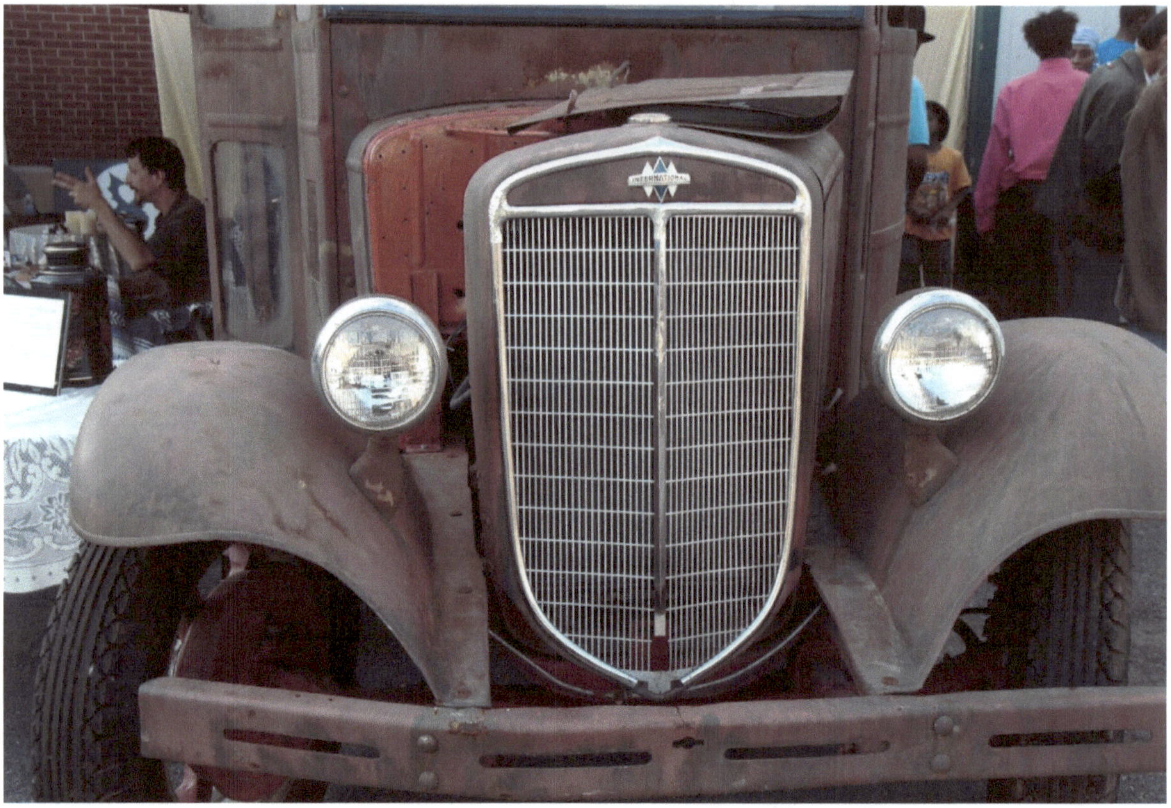

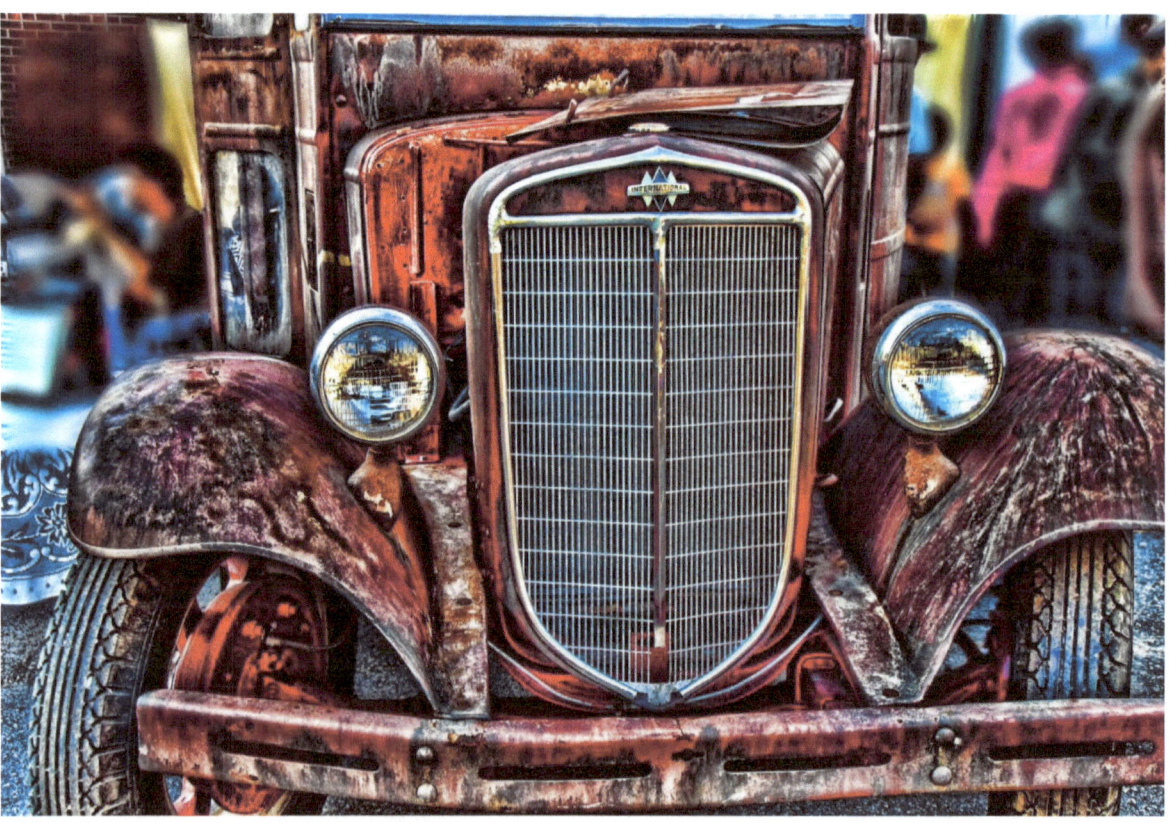

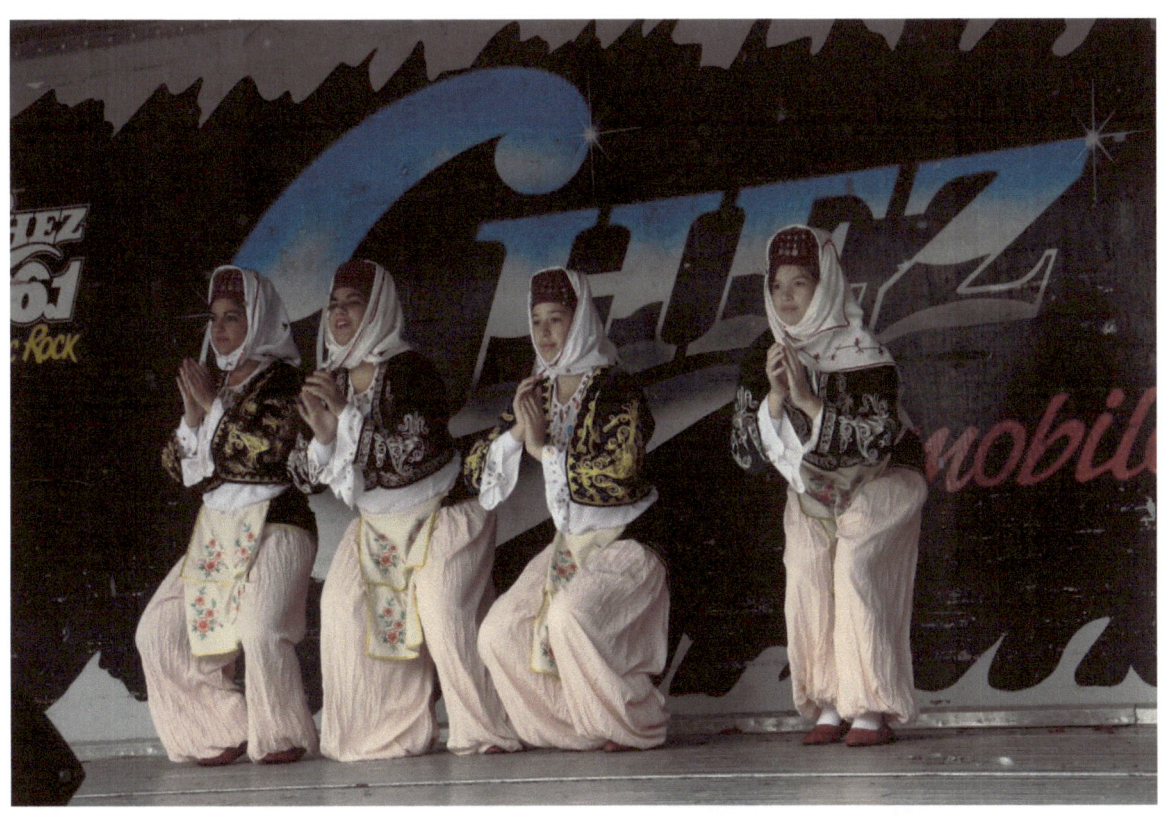

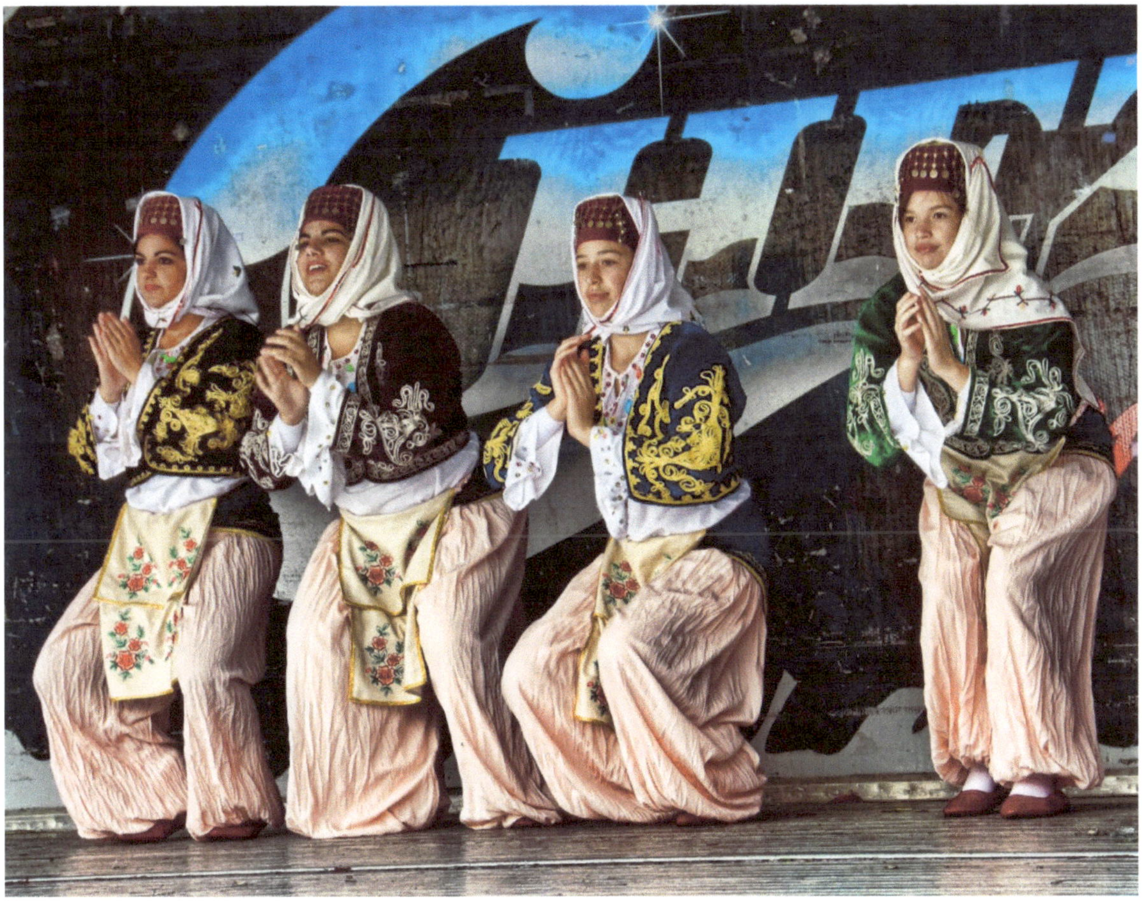

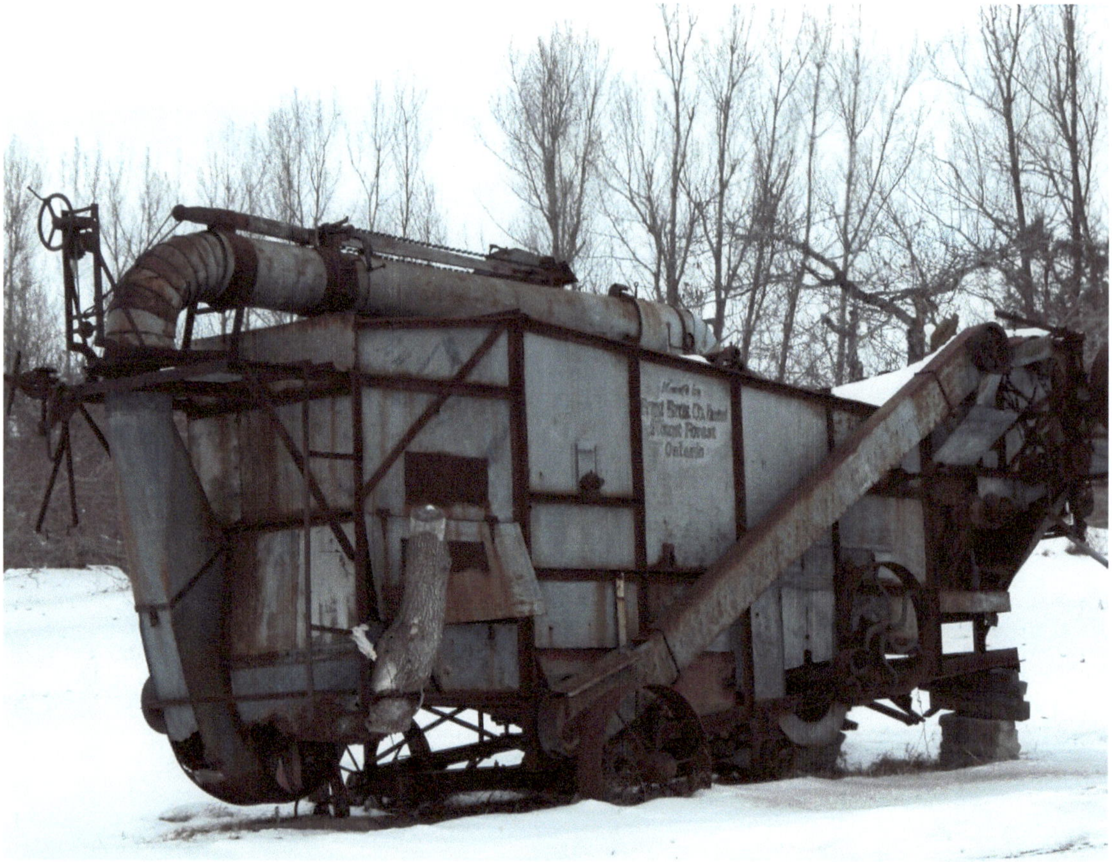
Ontario

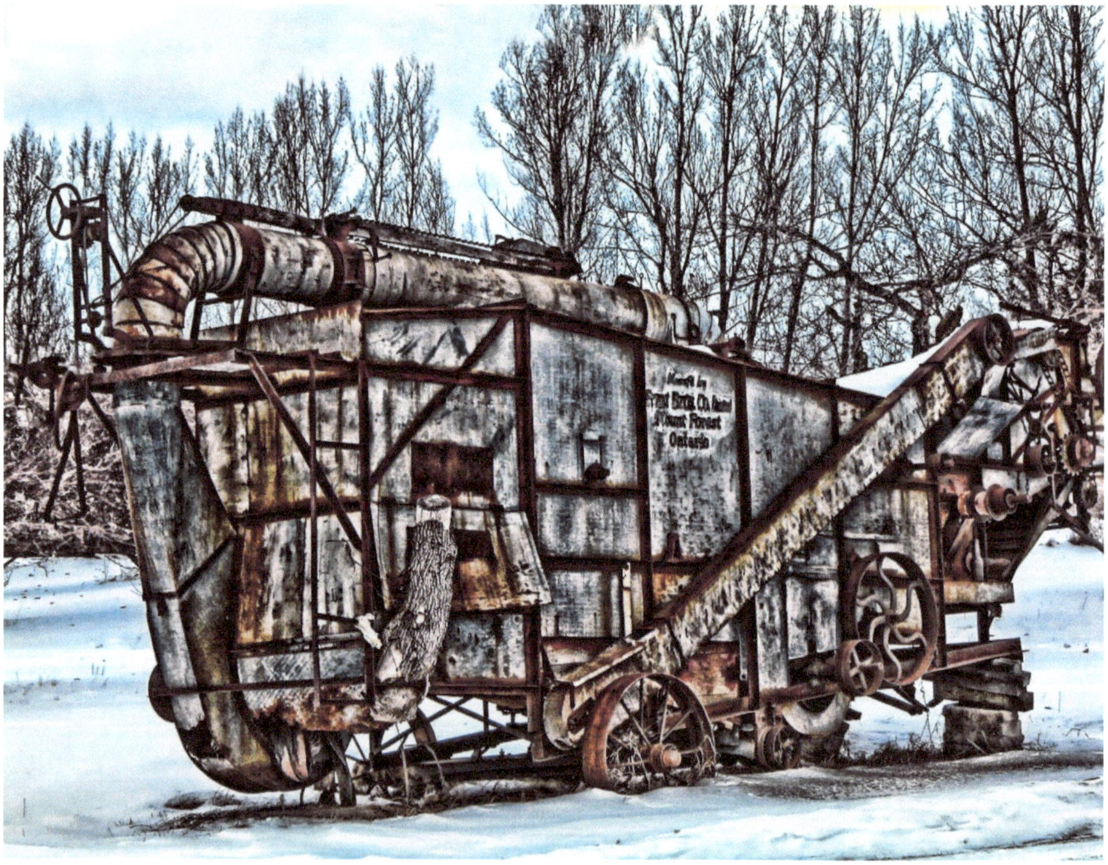
Ontario

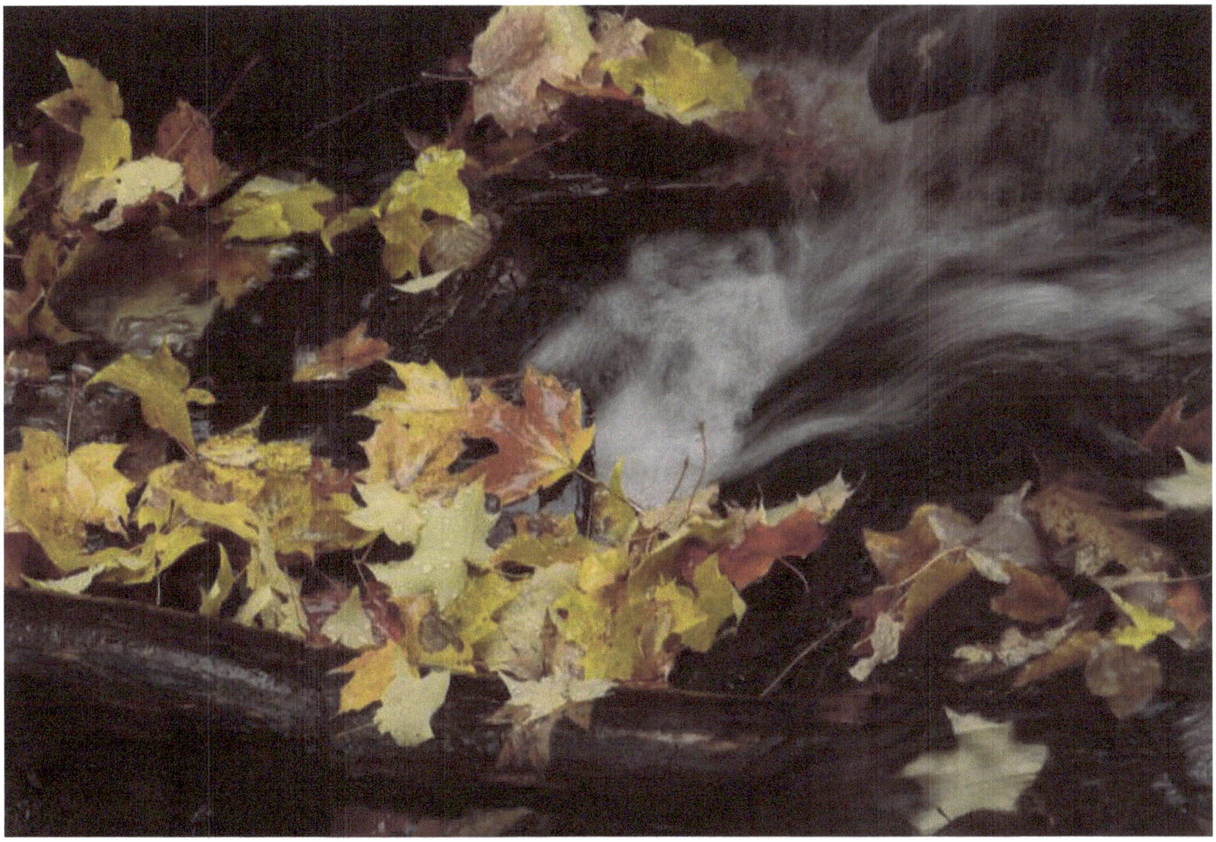

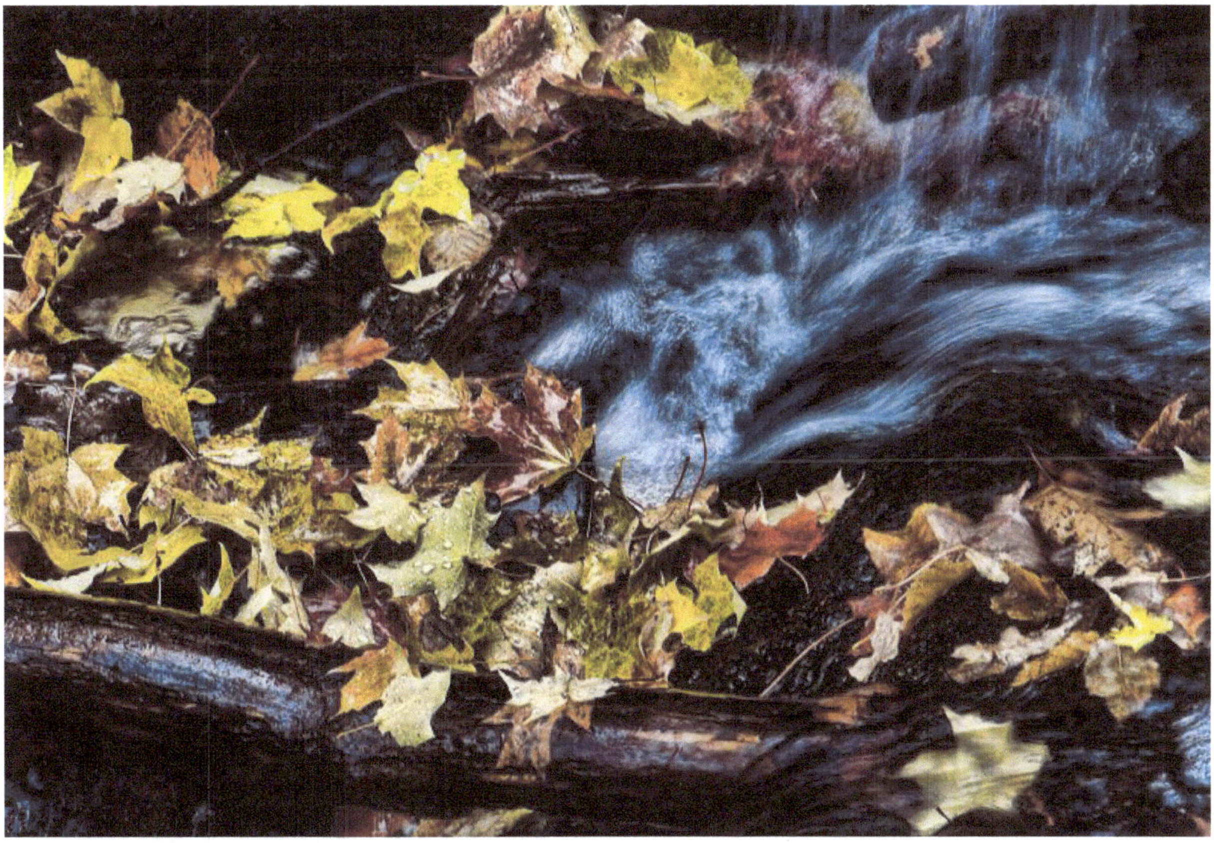

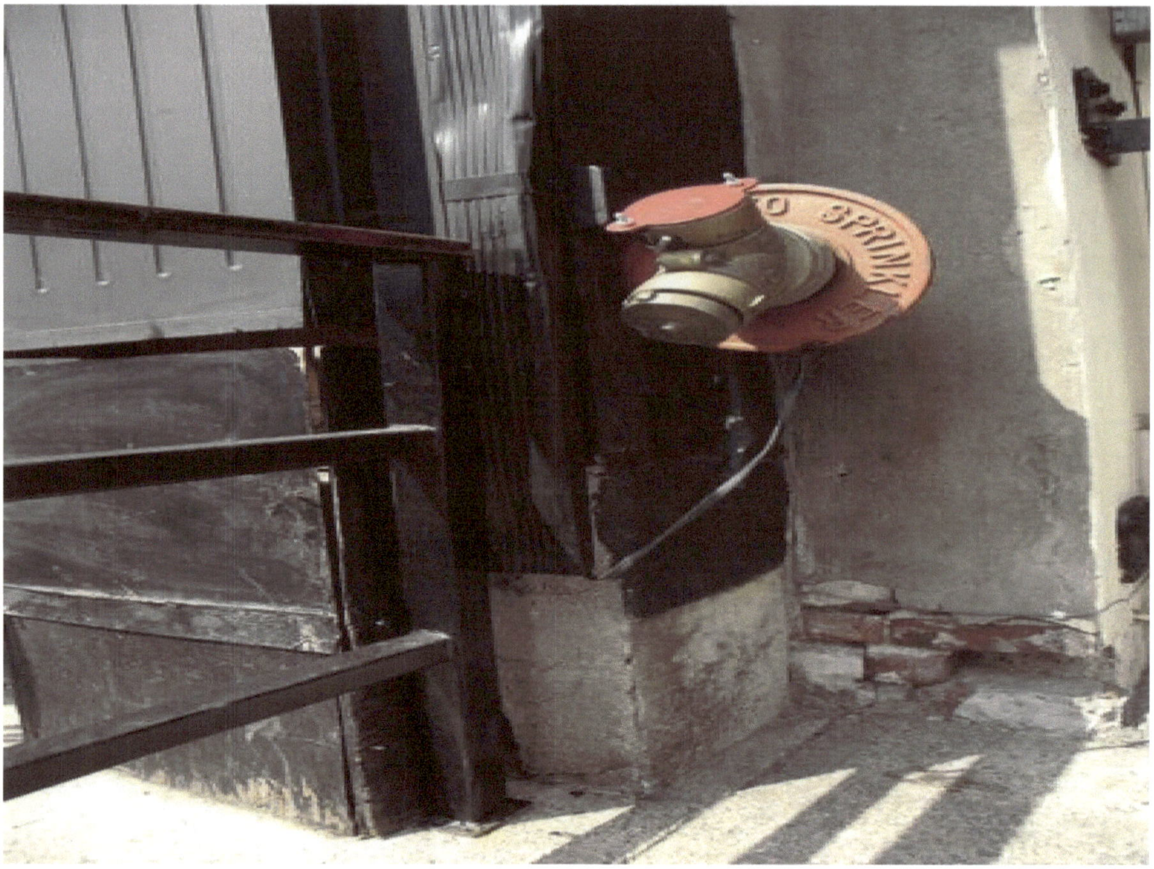
O SPRINKLER

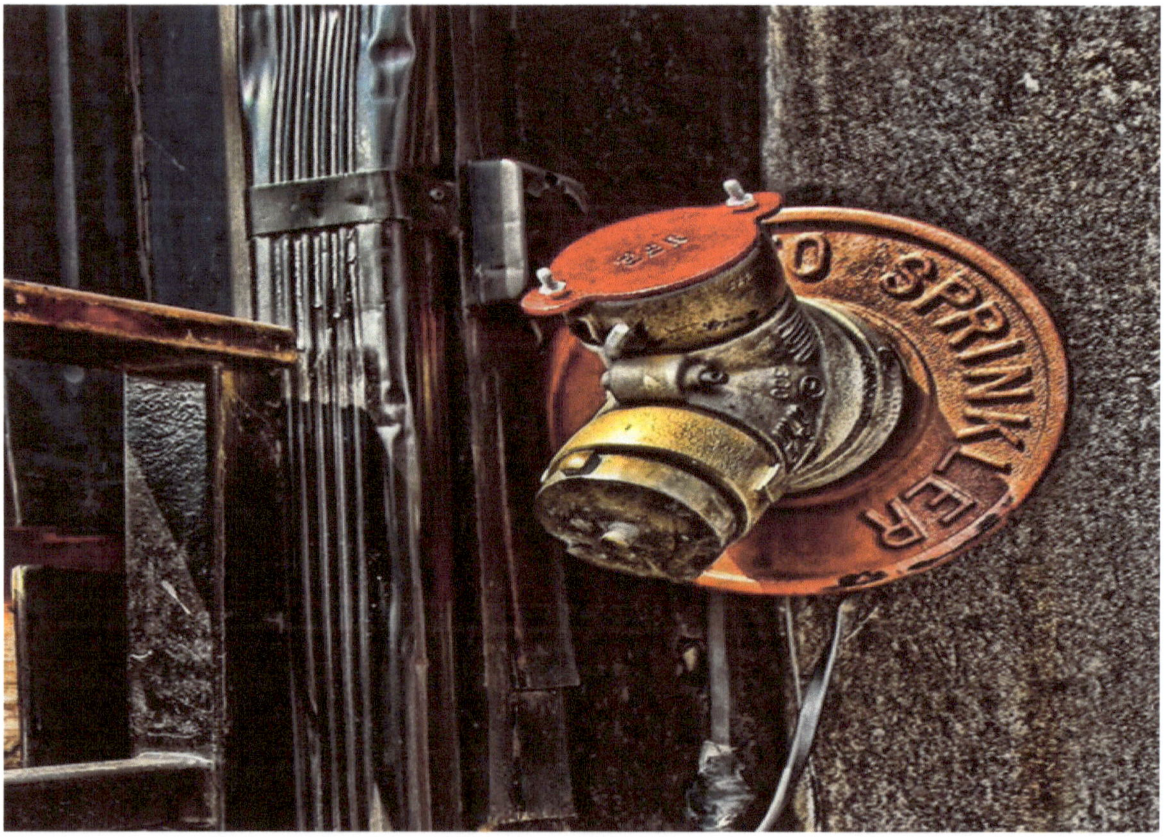
O SPRINKLER

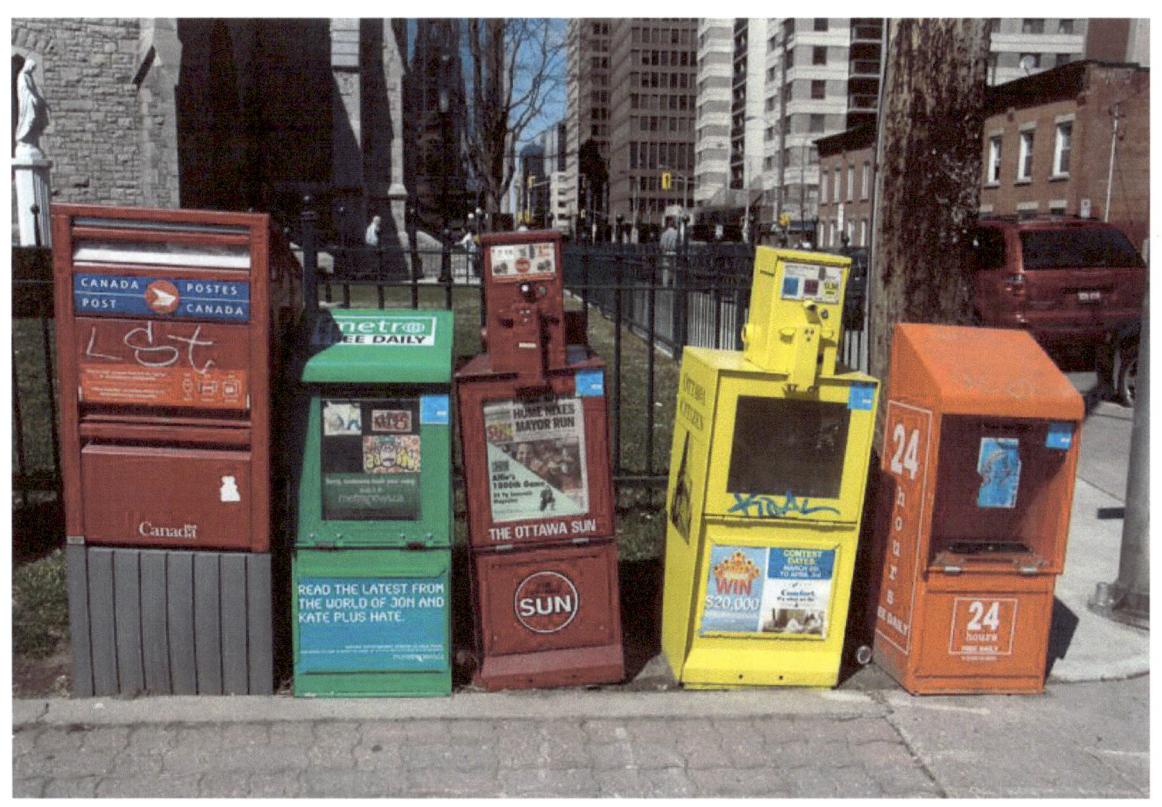

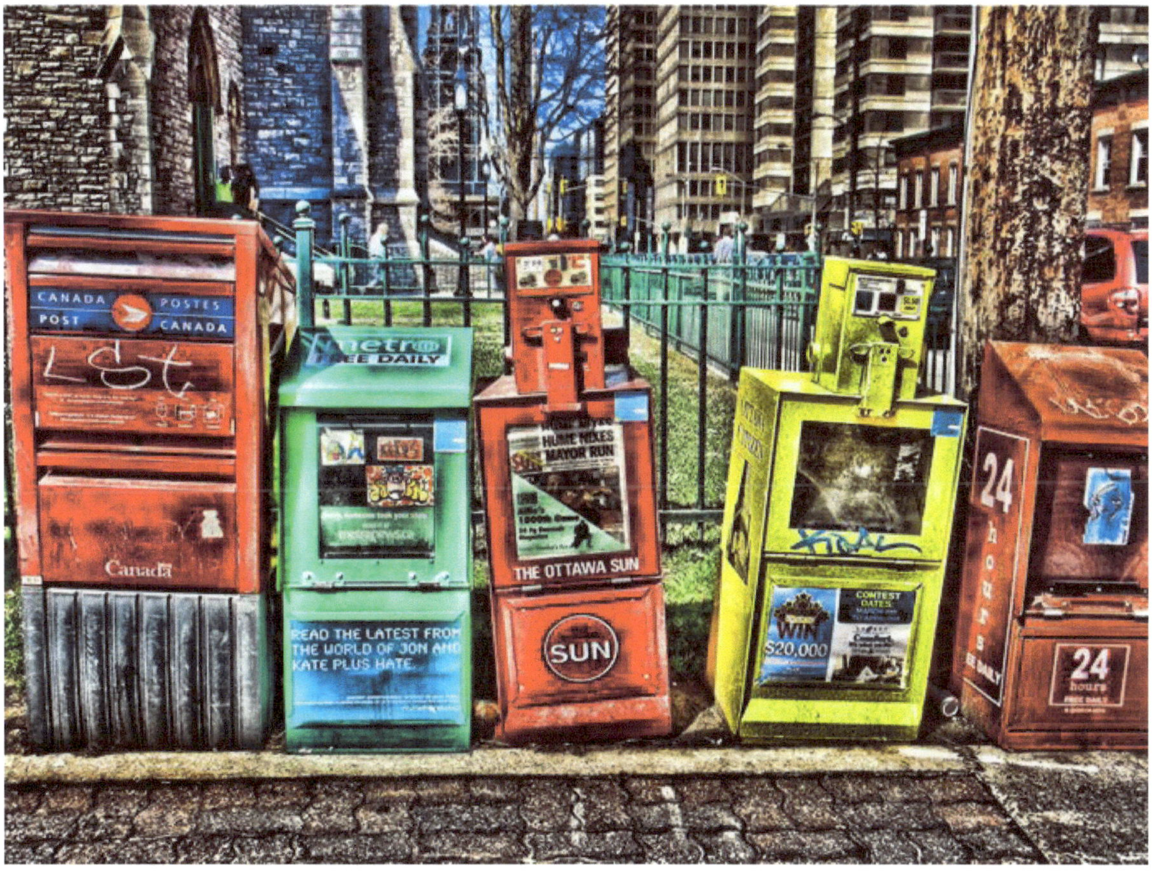

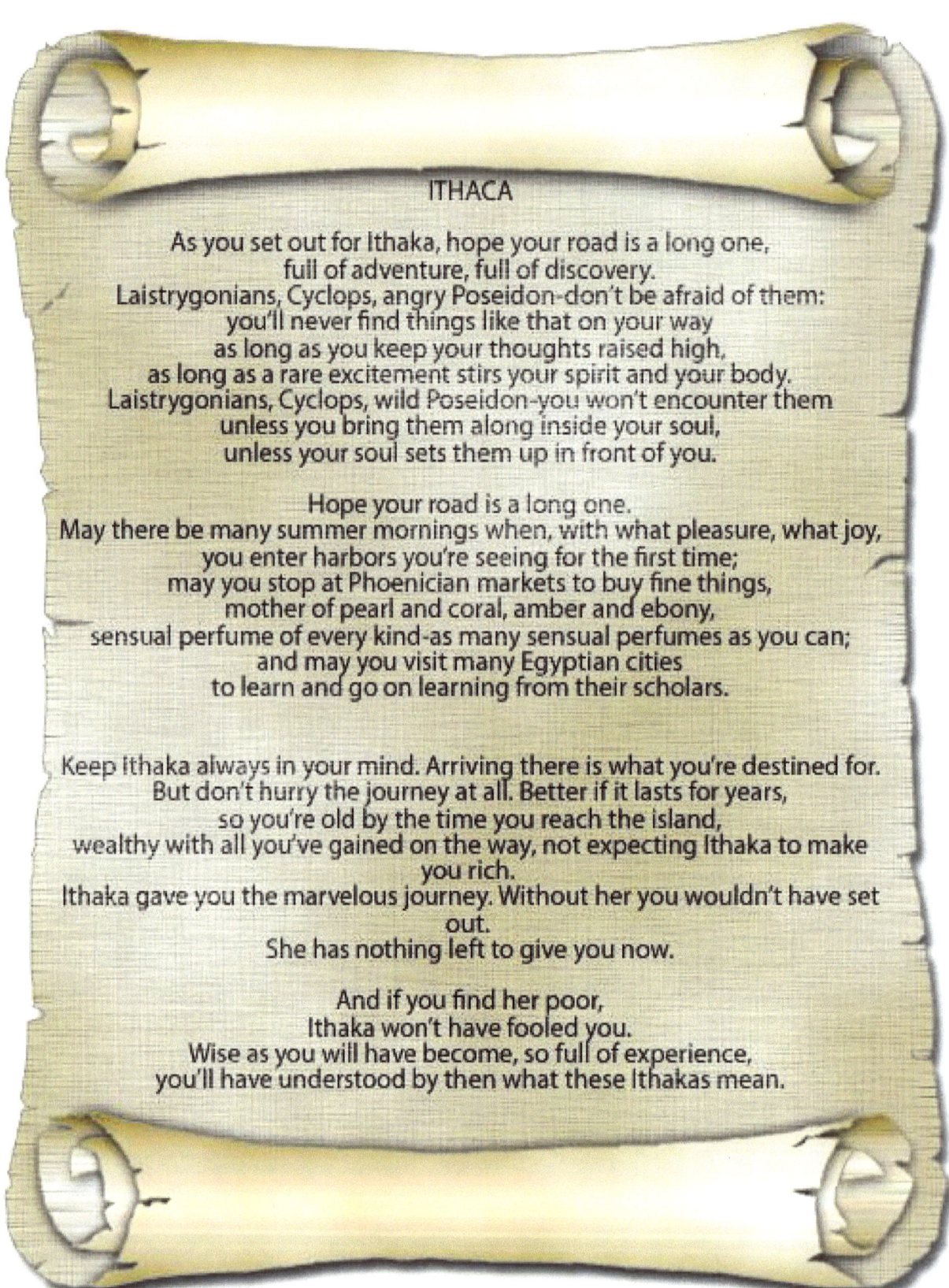

ITHACA

As you set out for Ithaka, hope your road is a long one,
full of adventure, full of discovery.
Laistrygonians, Cyclops, angry Poseidon-don't be afraid of them:
you'll never find things like that on your way
as long as you keep your thoughts raised high,
as long as a rare excitement stirs your spirit and your body.
Laistrygonians, Cyclops, wild Poseidon-you won't encounter them
unless you bring them along inside your soul,
unless your soul sets them up in front of you.

Hope your road is a long one.
May there be many summer mornings when, with what pleasure, what joy,
you enter harbors you're seeing for the first time;
may you stop at Phoenician markets to buy fine things,
mother of pearl and coral, amber and ebony,
sensual perfume of every kind-as many sensual perfumes as you can;
and may you visit many Egyptian cities
to learn and go on learning from their scholars.

Keep Ithaka always in your mind. Arriving there is what you're destined for.
But don't hurry the journey at all. Better if it lasts for years,
so you're old by the time you reach the island,
wealthy with all you've gained on the way, not expecting Ithaka to make
you rich.
Ithaka gave you the marvelous journey. Without her you wouldn't have set
out.
She has nothing left to give you now.

And if you find her poor,
Ithaka won't have fooled you.
Wise as you will have become, so full of experience,
you'll have understood by then what these Ithakas mean.

Panos FX, Scroll